OUTLINE OF
A
JUNGIAN
AESTHETICS

OUTLINE OF
A
JUNGIAN
AESTHETICS

BY

Morris Philipson

Northwestern University Press

1 9 6 3

FOR

TOLBIE & HARRY SACHER

*"Things excellent are as difficult
as they are rare."*

Preface

The intention of this study is to inquire into the accessibility of the ideas of C. G. Jung's psychology for the problems of aesthetics. While it is true that an increasing number of critics—for example, Maud Bodkin, Sir Herbert Read, and Wingfield Digby in England; Leslie Fiedler, Theodora Ward, and Walter Abell in the United States—have made use of various principles of Jung's thought for their practice of criticism, the fact remains that there is no thorough examination available of Jung's own writings specifically directed to this end.

The purpose of this "outline" is to present such an inquiry into Jung's work both systematically and critically.

In order to accomplish this, the investigation has been constructed in the following way. In the *Introduction*, a brief statement is made concerning the present state of relations between psychoanalytic thought and aesthetics; the historical development of the relationship between Jung and the Freudian school is indicated; and Jung's "image of man" is sketched in order to characterize the general nature of his thought relevant to aesthetics.

Since his theory of symbolism is the "middle term" between Jung's psychology and his reflections on art, *Part I* is concerned with setting forth Jung's interpretation of the nature of symbolism. This is drawn from a variety of his writings, from contexts by no means necessarily directed to the philosophy of art proper. The intention has been to offer these ideas as he himself presents and exemplifies them, which requires an exposition of much of Jung's general psychology, as well as critical comparisions with certain philosophical interpretations of symbolism.

Part II represents the implications that Jung himself draws from his psychology for the philosophy of art. The exposition involves contrasting his position with that of Freud's aesthetics, and remaining faithful to the limited examination Jung has made of aesthetic questions. I have refrained from drawing implications from Jung's works on religion and alchemy which, despite the fact that they exhibit "overlapping" or common concerns, would shift the focus away from problems of art.

It is in *Part III* that my conclusions are drawn and a critical examination is made of the previous systematic presentations. Such criticism is undertaken from the point of view of (1) conflicting psychoanalytic thought and in the light of current (2) anthropological, (3) literary, and (4) cultural historians' theories. The implications of Jung's contributions to aesthetics are evaluated, and, lastly, the lines for possible development of epistemology are indicated, consistent with the suggestions of Jung's psychology.

I wish to acknowledge here my appreciation for the critical readings of the manuscript, throughout its various stages of preparation, especially to Professor Albert Hofstadter and, also, to Professors Justus Buchler, Robert Gorham Davis, and Meyer Schapiro, all of Columbia University; and my gratitude for her help to the librarian of the Analytical Psychology Club of New York City.

M.P.

Contents

ix

PART II

PART III

Introduction

Jung's Image *of* Man

In order to discover something of what has been accomplished by the application of psychoanalytic thought to
the problems of art, if one reads through the anthology
Art and Psychoanalysis,[1] edited by William Phillips, it is
more than a little disappointing to recognize that Mr.
Phillips' introduction is nothing but a declaration of bank-
ruptcy. The great majority of essays included in the
volume are concerned with the influence of Freudian
thought on aesthetics, the psychology of artists, and practical criticism. Only two of the twenty-six essays refer to
the psychology of C. G. Jung in other than pejorative
language; and these two, strikingly enough, are not men-
tioned in the introduction.

3

Mr. Phillips, apparently, comes to the sad and distressing conclusion that (Freudian) psychoanalysis has led critics and aestheticians into more blind alleys than into green pastures. His summary statement, which he calls a paradox, reads as follows:

> The work of neurotic writers can be characterized as neurotic only by reducing its total meaning to its seemingly neurotic components—which, in turn, are assumed to be identical with the neurosis of the author.

It is this assumption—that the "total meaning" of the work of art can be so reductively interpreted on the basis of Freudian principles and methods—which has proved to be a Medusa's head rather than an aid to aesthetics. The so-called "paradox" revolves about the questions of (1) whether the art work is "nothing but" an expression of the artist's neurosis, and (2) whether the "total meaning" is to be equated with an analytic interpretation of such a neurosis. Numerous writers sympathetic to Freudian psychology have taken great pains to dispute both of these points, and much of their respectful criticism consists in withdrawing support from these contentions of Freud's. Professor Lionel Trilling, for example, has written persuasively against the former principle; psychoanalysts such as Ernst Kris and critics such as Kenneth Burke have conceded limitation to the latter.

But, it seems to me, only those writers who have taken the position of Jung into consideration have gone beyond this one-step-forward, two-steps-backward development.

4

The essay by Leslie Fiedler and that by Stanley Edgar Hyman present positions that seem more hopeful of the value that psychoanalytic theory may have for aesthetics and criticism, because they see in Jung's writing a defense of the analytic gains without indefensible overextension of scope. It is *not* the consequence of Jung's thought that the work of art should be treated as expressing a neurosis, which then should be "analyzed" as if it were the artist. Nor is it Jung's contention that the "total meaning" of the work of art is to be reduced to the individual artist's psychology. The art-work must not be treated as a transparency through which one looks into the past of the artist—not because such an interpretation is impossible, but because it is not as valuable (it does not tell us as much about *the work of art*) as the "prospective" value of a "synthetic" interpretation can. But this is to anticipate.

It would be useful, at this point, to indicate Jung's place in the psychoanalytic movement. He was born in Kesswil, Switzerland, on July 26, 1875. He took his medical degree in Basel, and in 1900 began his career as a psychiatrist, assisting Eugen Bleuler at the Burghölzli Mental Hospital in Zürich. With the exception of a period of study under Janet in Paris, during 1902, he remained in Zürich, becoming senior staff physician at the Psychiatric Clinic of Zürich University and Bleuler's collaborator. His first published paper, a development of his doctoral dissertation, entitled "On the Psychology and Pathology of So-called Occult Phenomena," appeared in 1902. During this period, he worked with newly developed Association Tests in order to confirm experimentally some of the early theoretical findings of Freud. As a champion of Freud's work, he was invited to meet the members of the first Psycho-Analytical Society in Vienna. According to Ernest Jones, Jung was a guest of the Society for the first time on March 6, 1907.[2] The meeting led to several years of close friendship with Freud and a fruitful intellectual exchange between the two. Jung became the editor of Freud and Bleuler's *Jahrbuch für psychoanalytische und psychopathologische Forschungen* and, in 1911, founded the International Psychoanalytic Society, of which he was elected the first president.

However, Jung's individual development led to his criticsm of Freud's general theory in the book *Wandlungen und Symbole der Libido*, published in 1912, and their differences of opinion led to a final break between Jung and the Vienna school in 1913. Ernest Jones records that Freud was eager to read the new work of Jung, but then Freud "wrote saying he could tell me the very page where Jung went wrong . . . ; having discovered that, he had lost further interest."[3] The biographer, also, quotes from a letter dated January 1, 1913, in which Freud writes, "Jung is crazy, but I don't really want a split; I should prefer him to leave his own accord."[4]

Jung has, since that time, been considered by Freudians as a dissenter from the "true" body of psychoanalysis, and his theories a regression to earlier modes of psychological thinking. Edward Glover, for example, considers that Jung's school of thought is nothing but a "throw-back" to pre-Freudian conscious psychology. Surely, the difference between Jung's and Freud's conceptions of the nature of the unconscious determine their subsequently

6

contrasting principles of explanation and methods of interpretation. Were this a work of comparative psychology,
those differences would be the center of the examination.
But here, it will be assumed that the reader is already
familiar with Freudian conceptions and constructs, and
they will be referred to only insofar as they are necessary
to point up the Jungian position by contrast, or to support it by comparison.

Throughout, it will be Jung's *image of man* which
stands as touchstone for his consequent reflections on the
nature of symbols and his suggestions concerning the
nature of art. It is Jung's conception of man, as a whole
and at his best, that will be briefly outlined here (in anticipation of further elaboration in the body of the work)
in order to place his ideas concerning the topics on which
this examination will focus.

The most important concept that psychoanalysis has
introduced into the psychology of human beings as a
"whole" is that of the *unconscious*. In contrast with most
previous considerations of the subject matter, reason and
irrationality, experienced consciously, are no longer considered exhaustive for a theory of the human psyche. If
it is understood that the Greek and the Rationalistic
formulations of *the health of the psyche* were expressed
so that, at its best, reason was seen to "rule" the irrational;
and the Christian and Romantic formulations were that
the irrational must bring "the light," must guide; then it
may be said that in Jung's analytic psychology, "wholeness" is imagined, at its best, as a continuing process in
which both the rational and the irrational *of consciousness*

7

are only a part of the elements. It is, rather, between the conscious and the unconscious that wholeness is brought about, and not by one dominating the other, but by a reciprocal interdependence.

In other words, to understand the individual as a "whole" requires that one grasps the primary anti-rationalistic concept that *ego-consciousness is not the center of psychic life*. Consciousness is not the moral "better" of that which is unconscious. On the other hand, in contrast to Christianity, no one particular form, no one tradition of symbols and images of the irrational or the unconscious has preference for all, or, for that matter, has prior rights over consciousness for anyone. Between the forces of consciousness and unconsciousness, the image of their relationship might be that of a democracy (not a Platonic "Republic" in which one functional class alone rules without a "loyal opposition"). It is precisely when an individual feels that the opposition within him is *not loyal* that he comes to know the experience of dis-integrating, losing wholeness. But there is no law of privilege as to which of the parties in the democracy may become the opposition without loyalty to the whole.

Jung's psychology makes the effort to work out, for the individual as a whole, an interpretation of the internal relationships between the conscious and unconscious factors in which the proper roles of both are accurately conceived. In this interpretation, neither consciousness nor the unconscious is the "preferred" member.

The necessity to pursue "wholeness" consciously is a consequence of experiencing the opposite of "wholeness" — disintegration. And the most crucial attacks against the

8

sense of being integrated come from manifestations of the unconscious. When this is experienced, for example, in dreams, visions, or fantasies which attack a given state of wholeness, the content of such manifestations is perceived as an image, and the effort to incorporate it into the on-going conscious process may go through the following stages: expression in symbolic language; the attempt to reduce the direct experience to a rational sequence, giving personal and impersonal origins; and the hope of assimilating the experience to the now revised whole of the personality.[5]

It is in this context that Jung discusses his interpretation of the *purpose* for which *images* come into being. Images are created "out of the primal stuff of revelation." For the one who has had the direct experience of a manifestation of the unconscious, the image functions as a *portrayal* of the first-hand event. Once such an image has been objectified, for others, its function is to "attract, to convince, to fascinate, and overpower," since, at the same time, images both "lead men to premonition while defending them against experience."

Thus, the double function of such images is introduced, namely, to contribute to consciousness something of the richness of the contents of the unconscious and, at the same time, to protect consciousness against being over-whelmed by the unconscious. The subject of concern for both this attraction and defense is the sanity of one's psychic life, the health of the individual as a whole.

To conceive of this psychical experience, one might imagine a spectrum that has the following appearance.

9

Unconscious life	/	Conscious life

←——————————————————————→

Chaos: the fluid rich- ness of immediate experience without order. The psyche without defense.	Barrenness: rigid order from which mean- ingfullness has disap- peared. The psyche "over-defended."

Between these two equally undesirable *extremes*, lies the field of the search for *"effective images,"* for sanity which is not bought at the price of sterility, nor immediate experience of the unconscious at the price of psychosis. "Effective images" are interpreted to function as the media through which manifestations of the unconscious can be transformed so that rich but chaotic contents may be assimilated into an ordered but fruitful sanity. Traditions of religious and scientific as well as artistic "systems" are highly developed bodies of symbolic portrayals and protections. It is accommodation to such systems, as are made available to us in our particular cultures, which "test" our specific social adaptation. But such traditions are only the accumulated, progressively developed, objectifications of many individuals' searches for such "images" as were "effective" for them.

Jung sees the health of psychic life, individual wholeness, as possible within the range between the two extremes of the spectrum. At the one extreme, the inability to transform an "eruption" of the unconscious into a useful image leaves the person defenseless against the unconscious; at the other extreme, the elaborate order of traditional symbols "over-defends" the individual against first-hand experiences which alone would be proper to him. Jung's contention is that the search must be honest to the individual in his own relation with the unconscious, and not a purchase at second hand of another's system of symbols, even though that may be the most generally practiced possibility. But to pursue the former way, despite the fact that it may be more dangerous, is closer to the conditions for achieving one's best self — one's *own* best self. This "way" is what Jung calls the *"process of individuation."*

In other words, the function of images with symbolic value is to supply the means by which contents of the unconscious are transformed and assimilated for the progressive well-being of the psyche as a whole. Insofar as symbolic systems pass through historical stages, such images may go from a primitive order of objectification, through a fruitful elaborate system, to an otiose, jejune state in which the images of the system have lost their affective power. In the last condition, the individual is no longer protected against the "perils to his soul" by the socially available system of symbols. For example, when the religion in which he was raised ceases to function significantly for his psychic life, he is confronted with the necessity of "re-making" himself.

The process of individuation is the search for a pragmatic individual interpretation: for direct contact with the unconscious, steering the dangerous course between chaos and sterility. In effect, the individual "in search of effective images" — the symbols that satisfy his need for "wholeness" — recapitulates in his own development, now undertaken consciously, the structure of the unconscious development of the histories of cultures.

One can see that Jung offers here the basis of his theories of religion and of imaginative art implicit in his conception of individual psychology.

PART

I

The Concept *of* Symbol *in* Jung's Psychology

SECTION I: *Jung's Distinction between Signs and Symbols*

The link that connects Jung's theory of individual psychology to the considerations of aesthetics, and to the relations between aesthetics and epistemology, is found in Jung's persistent efforts to define and employ the concept of *symbol*. The point at which his attempt becomes most distinctive, and of particular interest to philosophy, consequently, is with the distinction by which he separates himself from Freud's position and tries to go beyond it.

Writing in 1922, Jung states the contrast in the following manner:

> The essential factor of Freud's reductive method consists in the fact, that it collects all the circumstantial evidence of the unconscious backgrounds,

15

and, through the analysis and interpretation of this material, reconstructs the elementary, unconscious, instinctive processes. Those conscious contents which give us a clue, as it were, to the unconscious backgrounds are by Freud incorrectly termed symbols. These are not true symbols, however, since, according to his teaching, they have merely the role of signs or symptoms of the background processes.[1]

The point at issue is this: only if the Freudian general theoretical structure, to which the mainifest content of the "signs or symptoms" are reduced, were to be proved adequate—would the Freudian lumping together of signs and symbols be justified. Jung takes exception to this "adequacy." In effect, the Freudian assumption is that all symbolic content is susceptible of reduction to "the elementary . . . processes"; and that the structures of these processes are known.

Jung's opposition to this, first announced in his *Psychology of the Unconscious*, 1917, amounts to saying that (a) Freud's psychology of instinctual processes does not go far enough, because it is *not* the case that the class of *all* physic expressions is the creation of the personal unconscious; and (b) Freud's reductive method of analysis is not adequate, because such a system of explanation as "explains away" has not proved itself appropriate for the analysis of two classes of content which are essentially different. This is not at all to say that Jung considers Freud's theory and method totally wrong. As far as the "signs" of one's *personal* unconscious activity are concerned, Jung is in agreement with Freud. Jung writes, in cases where:

> ... libido is not converted into effective work, but
> flows away unconsciously along the old channel. ...
> Accordingly the patient remains at war with himself,
> in other words, neurotic. In such a case analysis in the
> strict sense of the word is indicated—that is, the
> reductive method inaugurated by Freud, whereby all
> inappropriate symbols are split up and reduced to
> their natural elements.[2]

But the division between these two analysts begins
with Jung's characterization of such unconscious content
as he calls *collective*. This concept, as such, will be examined intensively later, but for our purposes at this point
it should be only acknowledged that, with the introduction of the collective unconscious, Jung establishes a new
category to describe the source of a certain class of
psychic activity and this requires his reinterpretation of
the idea of the symbolic nature of conscious content.

Consequently, Jung contrasts the signs or symptoms
of the personal unconscious with what he considers dis-
tinctively symbolic.

> The true symbol differs essentially from this
> [symptoms], and should be understood as the ex-
> pression of an intuitive perception which can as yet,
> neither be apprehended better, nor expressed dif-
> ferently.[3]

In an even earlier paper entitled *The Transcendent
Function*, written in 1916, Jung had expressed it in the
following way: the new method of interpretation he is

describing ".... is based on the fact that the symbol (i.e., the dream picture or fantasy), is no longer evaluated *semiotically*, as a sign for the elementary instinctual processes, but really *symbolically*, whereby the word 'symbol' is taken to mean the best possible expression of a complex fact not yet clearly grasped by consciousness."

If the structure of the collective unconscious is not or can not be known or even posited to the same extent as the structure of the personal unconscious, then only those expressions that are reducible are "signs or symptoms"; whereas, those that are not reducible—to what Freud considered the elementary instinctual processes—must be recognized as *symbols* properly so called. The whole question rests on the criteria by which the referents of symptomatic or symbolic expressions are identified. The structure of the personal unconscious is, in Freudian psychology, assumed to be known. The structure of the collective unconscious—to which Jung argues the truly symbolic expressions refer—is not equally well known, at this stage.

Again, in an essay called *On Psychical Energy*, 1928, Jung remarks:

> Far be it from me to assert that the semiotic interpretation is meaningless; it is not only possible, but also very true. Its usefulness is undisputed in all those cases where nature is merely crippled, without any effective accomplishment coming from it. But the semiotic interpretation becomes meaningless when it is applied exclusively and schematically, when, in short, it ignores the real nature of the symbol and

seeks to depreciate it to the level of a mere sign.

The symbol, then, is something which achieves an "effective accomplishment" as contrasted with a sign which functions only as the expression of a psychological "dead end." In these remarks, one begins to see emerging in Jung's thought the contrast that develops into the distinction between psychological functions in the service of Nature or Life, and those in the service of Culture or Spirit. That there is a conflict between these two principles goes without saying; but, for Jung, a psychology based on either, without sufficient understanding of the other, is unbalanced and inadequate to human beings.

Thus, the principle which Jung has put into question is the Freudian assumption that *all* "symbolic" expressions can be reduced to the structure of the personal unconscious. If the Freudian position were adequate, then it would follow that all non-literal expressions—particularly, in the light of our ultimate consideration here: all *artworks*—are reducible to the fundamental instinctual processes, namely, of the libido. But Jung opposes this assumption in the effort to save such content as characterizes culture, most especially religion and art, from being reduced to (i.e., "explained away" by) a causally reductive analysis in the one-sided service of Nature.

The reduction of a symptom in order to make possible the fulfillment of a natural need is necessary for the treatment of neuroses. But, Jung argues, the identification of all psychical expressions with the class of neurotic symptoms is "illegitimate" — empirically indefensible. "If the natural were really the ideal condition," Jung writes,

"then the primitive would be leading an enviable existence. But that is by no means so, for ... the primitive is
tortured by superstitions, anxieties, and compulsions. ..."

Certainly the goal of psychoanalytic therapy is to re-
store a psyche to a state of health, and this is associated
with the condition called "natural." But Jung's argument
rests on the attitude that the natural life is not only good
in itself, but good in that it makes a psyche free for what
he calls "effective accomplishment"—primary among
which are science, art, and religion. Were these to be
mistaken for by-products of neurotic repression, then all
culture would be misunderstood as "substitute gratification." Jung maintains that culture is no substitute for
natural gratification; the function it serves in the economy
of the psyche is not to be explained by reduction. The
source of genuine symbols is in that quantum of psychical
energy which is in excess of that needed for instinctual
gratification.

> Just as in physical Nature, only a very small por-
> tion of the natural energy can be transformed into
> practically useful energy, and by far the greater part
> must be left to work itself out in natural phenomena,
> so in our psychical Nature, only a small part of the
> total energy can be drawn away from the natural
> flow.... Therefore, the libido is by nature appor-
> tioned out to the various function-systems from
> which it cannot be wholly withdrawn.... Only in a
> case where a symbol offers a greater potential than
> nature, is it possible to convert the libido into other
> forms.... The fact that the symbol makes this de-

flection of energy possible shows that not all the libido is bound up in a form determined by natural law whereby a regular course is enforced, but that a certain quantum of energy remains over, and may be termed excess libido.[4]

Jung then uses the simile of a waterpipe system for the various natural function-systems and compares the libido with the quantity of water flowing through it. If, he posits, the size of the pipes is not large enough to handle the intensity of a flow, then the "overflow" of libido, the excess, is available for a use other than that of the "natural" system, i.e., is capable of transformation.

> From this excess of libido certain psychical processes result which cannot be explained, or only very inadequately explained, by mere natural conditions. How are we to explain the religious processes, for instance, the nature of which is essentially symbolical? In the form of representations, symbols are religious ideas; in the form of action, they are rites or ceremonies. Symbols are the manifestation and expression of the excess libido. At the same time, they are transitions to new activities, which must be specifically characterized as cultural activities in contrast to the instinctive functions that run their course according to natural law.

In other words, symbols "represent" (show forth), somehow embody an excess of libido over and above that necessary to the natural system, whereas symptoms "represent" (manifest) blockages within the natural system. The fact that both symptoms and symbols are expressed by non-literal, non-discursive means is what leads to the Freudian confusion of the two. But Jung sees the symbol as functioning directly in the service of the principle of Spirit or Culture in contrast with the symptom which functions indirectly in the service of Nature. He writes:

> Only in a case where a symbol offers a greater potential than nature, is it possible to convert the libido into other forms. The history of culture has sufficiently demonstrated that man possesses a relative superfluity of energy which is capable of application over and above the merely natural flow.

It may be seen that, even in this mechanical model for the idea of psychical energy, libido is identified with the unconscious source of psychical activity. The distinction has not been maintained here between the personal and the collective unconscious, and the model would become rather awkward for much further metaphorical elaboration. But it is worthwhile for summing up Jung's idea of the symbol at this stage of his considerations.

> We have every reason to value the making of symbols, he writes, and to tender our homage to the symbol as the invaluable means by which we are able to use for effective work the merely instinctive flow of the energic process. . . .
> The transformation of libido through the symbol is a process that has been taking place since the beginning of time and its effectiveness continues.

22

> Symbols are never thought out consciously; they are always produced from the unconscious in the way of so-called revelation, or intuition.

The crux of the matter seems to be a contrast between symptoms and symbols in terms of purpose, or final cause. *Symptoms* are expressions of a disfunction in the natural system. Insofar as they are not understood, they may present a moral problem for an individual or a society; but insofar as they are interpreted analytically they become the "clues" for possible treatment toward cure. *Symbols* are expressions of a function in the economy of the libido which enables the individual or a sociey to turn excess psychical energy to "effective accomplishment." Thus the symbol appears as a "lure" which enables psychical energy to be transformed into achievements of an aesthetic, religious, scientific, or social value.

As to the material cause of the symbol, at this stage of his development, Jung writes:

> Inasmuch as "no created mind can penetrate the inner soul of Nature," you will surely not expect the impossible of our psychology, namely, a valid explanation of that great mystery of life, that we immediately feel in the creative impulse. Like every other science, psychology has only a modest contribution to make towards the better and deeper understanding of life; it is no nearer than its sisters to absolute knowledge.

As to the efficient cause of the symbol, Jung writes:

> Judging from the close relation of the mytholog-

ical symbol to the dream symbol, ... it is more than probable that the greater part of the historical symbols arise directly from dreams, or at least are inspired by them.

The formal cause of the symbol is, thus, seen as such manifestations (images, fantasies, dreams, myths, etc.) as (1) express a complex fact not yet clearly grasped by consciousness, and, (2) thereby, deflect the energy of the libido to effective work above and beyond that needed for the maintenance of the natural system. The simplest manner in which this conception might be stated is that a symbol is a psychical *suggestion* of such *power* as to *make actual* that which is conceived as a *possibility*.

At this point it is well to consider certain interpretations of philological, literary, and philosophical writers concerning symbols, in order, subsequently, to compare and contrast these earlier statements of Jung with his own more fully developed position.

SECTION 2: *Critical Comparisons*

I should like to indicate a line of analysis of what Jung might have assumed concerning the concept of symbol. In ordinary usage, the word "symbol" is employed in superficially distinguishable modes. *The symbol is an artificial or a natural object which represents or stands for:*

  i. a class of a qualitative or conceptual nature, e.g. the peacock is a symbol of pride; the halo is a symbol of saintliness; etc.

  ii. another object, e.g., a word which is the name of a

24

person; a coat-of-arms which is the "outward sign" of a family; etc.

iii. a specific event or condition, e.g., a cross for the crucifixion of Jesus; graphic symbols for mathematical concepts; etc.

The difficulties which these uses of the word "symbol" disguise are pointed to by the questions of (1) what the logical relationship is between the symbol and its referent, as well as (2) the existential status of the referent.

In ordinary usage, it would appear that both the symbol and that which it represents are equally knowable. In effect, they would seem to have a relationship of logical equivalence; their "meaning" is the same. This would assume that the referent could be known as such, totally independent of any symbol for it. But that conception would appear to be closer to the stipulation for the use of the word "sign," as is demonstrated by the example of different natural languages in which different words stand for the same object or event. This ignores the more subtle problem of the concept of logical connectives, to say nothing of the problem of universals; but even in the more obvious instance of ordinary words or phrases which are *not* translatable, natural languages offer exceptions to the idea that the referents of the "symbols" can be known independent of any (or any special) representation. Untranslatable words or phrases stand as examples, for cultural history, that different expressions are representative of and comprehensible in only a specific context or environment. They do not have exact logical equivalance in any other semantical or syntactical system; no other written or spoken symbol can mean exactly the same as that in the original language, since no other environment can make the experience—to which it refers—possible.

Nevertheless, not only in respect to untranslatable verbal expressions, in the case of graphic or plastic or gestural symbols, as well, it is a common occurrence to mistake the symbol for its referent—where the referent is not an object or event which is known independent of any symbol. Kant's observation (that to have an idea is not the same as having the object of the idea) notwithstanding, ordinary experience frequently mistakes "possession" of the one for the other.

It appears, on closer inspection, therefore, that all three of the above categorized uses of the word "symbol" are suspect whenever (1) that which represents is logically equivalent to that which it represents, e.g., when arabic or roman numerals are used to "symbolize" numerical concepts; and (2) when the referent can be known independent of any particular symbol, e.g., when a person is "known" without his name, or a family is known without their coat-of-arms.

In either of the above classes, in other words, the natural or artificial object standing for something else is a *sign*. On Robinson Crusoe's island, footprints in the sand are "signs of life"; but that "man is made in the image of God," is a symbolic statement. A *symbol*, more strictly stipulated, thus, can be said to be (1) a representation which is *not* logically equivalent to that which it represents; and (2) the referent is not knowable except through the medium of *some* natural or artificial representation. It is not knowable directly. This latter condition, refers to the question of the existential status of the referent. It raises the issue of verification or confirmation insofar as it indicates that what is most typical of the class of symbols is that the referents are not available to such empirical tests as identify the objects of natural science.

Both signs and symbols share the structural relation to their referents of representing or standing for. But symbols are distinguished from signs on the basis of the functional relation of making, at least partly, known that which would be otherwise unknowable. Again, to put it as simply as possible: *signs* appear to be representations of specific, known or knowable, referents, whereas, *symbols* appear to be representations of otherwise unspecified or otherwise unknown referents.

This contrast seems to be perfectly consistent with philological explanations of the origins of the Greek root word for "symbol."

In Greek, the word is *symbolon*. It is constituted of the syllable *syn*, which means "together, common, simultaneous with, or according to," and the word *bolon*, which means "that which has been thrown"; coming from the verb form *ballo*, "I throw." When the object called a "symbol" is thought of independent from what it represents, the implication is drawn that it is constituted of elements that have been thrown together.

But the etymological implications are more subtle than that. "Symbol" means something perceptible which results from an activity of throwing together such things as have something in common — between that which represents and that to which it refers. It may be translated as a token, a pledge, a premonitory sign, a distinctive mark, or an adumbration. According to the studies of

Bryson, Finkelstein, MacIver, and McKeon,[5] the Greeks understood by "symbol" a *tally*. That is, a half of a bone or coin or other object which two parties broke between them in order to have proof of identity. When fitted together, the two parts of the tally made a whole. Should someone come into possession of one part of such a "tally," his part would be for him the familiar or known; whereas, the part which is not familiar to him, which would make it a whole, that part which is still unknown is, literally, the uncanny. The symbol, thus, is part of an attempt to link a given known with an unknown; it is a content, available to senory perception which would connect present experience with something that is not immediately available.

In *The Nature of Thought*, B. Blanchard says, in describing the effect of symbols: "on the warrant of something given in sensation at the time, we unreflectingly take some object to be before us." In *The Heritage of Symbolism*, C. M. Bowra discusses the "joining" experience which the symbol achieves in a contrast of "worlds," so that the great symbolists are those who give us the exaltation and grandeur of that other world "there" while their feet are firmly set on the earth "here." In Charles Morris' view, the symbol is a section of an historical and social "field" which contains both the process of symbolizing, the apprehending individual, and the referent as well.[6]

In each of these theories, the symbol is interpreted primarily in respect to its function as a tally. The "broken-off part," that which is presently available, is not a totally independent entity, but, wherever it goes, "carries with it" and "points to" the whole in which it participated as well as the situation in which it was broken in half. When one experiences the "throwing together," i.e., when one has an insight into the missing part—the value of the whole is made manifest; through the symbol, one has come to discover this value of the whole. In this respect, the symbol does not create the value but conveys it as a key conveys possible entry into that which is hidden. The known is experienced as the "here"; the unknown as the "there." In *Decline of the West*, Spengler wrote: "We live in the 'here' as something of our own and experience the 'there' as something alien and uncannny."[7] Symbols, he argues, are charged with "dread, awe, reverence"—because, by an act which is both unconscious and creative, they throw a bridge between consciousness and the unconscious.

Consistent with these suggestive descriptions above one can speak of the "school of thought" with which Jung's treatment of symbolism is in harmony.

It should be undestood that, from the point of view of Freudian psychoanalytic theory, there is strong opposition to this interpretation. Otto Fenichel, for example, writes in *The Psychoanalytical Theory of Neurosis*, that while "the unconscious continually strives for expression . . . Also to be noted is the fact that everyone shares a common reservoir of expressions that serve to distort meaning—symbolism." He later goes on to say that such distortion is a "prelogical . . . an archaic way of perceiving the world" and in a developed civilization, its function is exclusively that of "a substitute for unpleasant reality"— not in any sense "an attempt to master reality."

Similar views are held by Rank, Sachs, and Jones—that symbols disguise repressed material. In the view of Ernest Jones, a symbol arises as the unconscious urge to express an idea, highly charged with feeling, which must be kept hidden. It fulfills the need to endow the external world with something of the self in order to make it recognizable and manageable. But he considers this a regression and, since the symbol "undersublimates," the activity fails of its purpose. Sharpe, Milner, Rycroft, and other British analysts treat the problem in a similar manner.

For our purposes, however, it is not in contrast with conflicting schools of analytic psychology that Jung's position can come to be most sharply appreciated; rather, it is the comparison with certain theological and philosophical writings—particularly those of Tillich, Langer, and Cassirer—which throws the most clearly revealing intellectual light upon it.

Ernst Cassirer makes much of the distinction between signs and symbols, and speaks of prelogical thinking, too. "Any one concrete and individual sign," he writes, "refers to a certain individual thing . . . [in contrast:] A genuine human symbol is characterized not by its uniformity but by its versatility."[8] His point there is that, while in early childhood and in primitive mentality there is a rigidity in the way that signs are related to their referents (i.e., where the relation is held to be one of logical equivalence) in more developed thought a symbol is something different from a sign, since the relation between the representation and its referent is not so simple. To call the symbol versatile is one way of saying that, independent of using it, we have no fixed idea of its referent. It is available to the ingenuity and versatility of interpreters precisely for this reason.

By distinguishing our experience of things from our experience of ideas, Cassirer argues, humanity gradually overcomes prelogical thinking. The development of logical thinking leads the epistemologist, subsequently, to examine "the dependence of relational thought upon symbolic thought." What he considers unique to human consciousness is the ability to isolate relations, that is, "to consider them in their abstract meaning." The objects of abstract reflections may be "fixed elements" singled out from "the stream of floating sensuous phenomena" but the process of singling out is achieved by symbols. Without symbolic thought, abstract reflection would be impossible.

> Without symbolism the life of man would be that of the prisoners in the cave of Plato's famous simile. Man's life would be confined within the limits of his biological needs and his practical interests; it could find no access to the "ideal world" which is open to him from different sides by religion, art, philosophy, science.

And again:

> It is symbolic thought which overcomes the natural inertia of man and endows him with a new ability, the ability constantly to reshape his human universe.

In writing critically of certain propositions concerning God, Professor Walter Kaufmann, in his *Critique of Religion and Philosophy*, calls on Cassirer for support, but, I believe, misinterprets Cassirer in the process. "As these words are generally used, both in ordinary language and by the most judicious writer," he says, "symbols no less than signs, and *Symbole* no less than *Zeichen,* stand for something specific, while propositions about God are essentially ambiguous."[9] Further, he writes: "... most ... religious propositions which are allegedly literally false but symbolically true are not symbols of some specifiable truth. They are ambiguous." And, in conclusion: "That the stories of *Genesis* are an inexhaustible fount of interpretations is no objection: it is this very quality that repays every return to the text. But if this rich ambiguity is irreducible and reappears covertly in theology, then the validity and worth-whileness of theology becomes questionable. We might prefer overt myths."

The conflict between spiritual experience, on the one hand, and theology, on the other, as Kaufmann examines it, is not our concern here; but the contrast between signs and symbols is. It is Kaufmann's position that, while symbols and signs should not be distinguished on the basis of their referents and their relations to such referents, he does make use, for his own purposes, of a contrast between such referents which are "specific" or "specifiable" and those which are "ambiguous" — "rich" therein (sic!) — and "irreducible."

What Kaufmann is arguing against is the position of Paul Tillich to the effect that "discourse about God" is to be construed as "symbolically true." Tillich's interpretation of the difference between signs and symbols makes a major point of his idea that "a genuine symbol participates in the reality of that which it symbolizes." But

Kaufmann considers this stipulation "extremely unclear. It sounds profound, but a moment's reflection will show that such 'participation' is very common and not in the least mysterious—nor particularly relevant to discourse about God."

Tillich believes that he is contributing to clarification of *knowledge* concerning God, while Kaufmann's criticism amounts to ranging argument against Tillich to the conclusion that Tillich's idea of religious propositions being called "symbolically *true*" means only that they are "richly ambiguous," which Kaufmann calls "true—but put very misleadingly."

However, in the writings of Cassirer, Langer, and Jung —it is not a question of "truth" which is foremost. They are each concerned, first, with distinguishing signs and symbols in order to characterize different conditions for the use or development of knowledge. The difference between them may be that Langer and Cassirer are concerned with epistemology, with the psychical process which is called rational thought, whereas Jung is concerned with the psychology of psychical functions in general, not all of which are rational. Therefore, Jung's use of symbol will have a wider scope. But, for the present, it is important to locate the common area of agreement in the interpretation of symbol by these philosophers and Jung.

Kaufmann covertly maintains the distinction between such representations as are signs or symbols while trying to say that these words have identical meanings. He maintains it by distinguishing between such representations as have specific referents and such referents as are ambig-

33

uous. At the same time, he insists that "Tillich's distinction between sign and symbol has no foundation in our language."

In contrast to his position, Susanne K. Langer, writes in *Philosophy in a New Key* (which is subtitled "A Study in the Symbolism of Reason, Rite, and Art"), concerning

> ... the genuine difference between sign and symbol. The sign is something to act upon, or a means to command action; the symbol is an instrument of thought."[10]

Consistent with Cassirer, Langer is saying that signs or signals are distinguished by the fact that their referents are specific things. Thus, they are known or knowable independent of any particular sign, but such knowledge is primarily a form of action. Symbols, on the other hand, while their referents may be "specifi*able*," do not have *things* as referents; and the object of the symbol could not possibly become known except through some representation.

> A term which is used symbolically and not signally does *not* evoke action appropriate to the presence of its object. ... Symbols are not proxy for their objects, but are *vehicles for the conception of objects.* ... In talking *about* things we have conceptions of them,, not the things themselves; and *it is the conceptions, not the things, that symbols directly "mean."*[11]

That the objects of symbols are *specifiable* would appear to make Mrs. Langer's statements consistent with

Professor Kaufmann's; but there is an appreciable differ-ence between saying that what may be specified as the referent is an object or the conception of an object. Lastly, what comes to the forefront in both Langer and Cassirer is that what has primary importance for rational thought is the conception of *relations* (i.e., events, proc-esses, conditions) rather than the conception of "objects." Again, while these two authors are especially concerned with rational thought and their examples are taken from the uses of abstract conceptions, when we compare Jung with Cassirer and Langer, it will be obvious that, in Jung's psychology, psychic functions in general, rational and irrational, and consequently art and religion, must be accounted for without a "prejudiced" primary concern with rational thought. It would be like saying: since *reason* is their major interest, Cassirer and Langer find rationality in the symbolism of rite and art as well as in science; whereas, since Jung's major interest is in psychi-cal *wholeness*, he finds symbolism not only in ritual and art but in rational thought as well. We are now in a posi-tion to consider the later, more developed, uses to which Jung puts his interpretation of symbols.

SECTION 3: *Symbols and Psychic Energy in the Service of "Wholeness"*

Jung asks: "does not all culture begin with the individ-ual?" and supports the "Yes" implicit in the rhetorical question by asserting that because "the things of the inner world influence us all the more powerfully for being

35

unconscious, it is essential for anyone who intends to make progress in self-culture to objectify the effects (of the unconscious) and then try to understand what contents underlie those effects."[12] Thus, the *objectification* of the *effects* of the *contents* of the *unconscious* are the data crucial to the formulation of Jung's theory of symbolism.

Insofar as such an intention is carried out by a patient in relation with a practitioner of analytic psychology, the process is therapy. But Jung conceives of therapy as only a stage in the continuing process of individuation. The goal is always the same, namely, mental health or "wholeness." But just as physical health is a process which must accommodate to both internal and external changes, so "wholeness" as a concept for mental health must be characterized by a *dynamics* (the study of the subject matter and methods that govern an activity) which extends beyond the doctor-patient relationship. As far as the individual is concerned, the "culture" which begins with the search for "self-cure," has as its intention that individual's "wholeness." But the methods by which it is achieved in the individual enable Jung to make descriptions, by extrapolation, of the nature of social as well as individual "culture."

The means to the end of "wholeness" are the methods by which libido is controlled. Such control becomes necessary when there is internal conflict—that is, when the individual consciousness is no longer "coupled together without differentiation" from the personal and collective unconscious, but, rather, suffers opposition between or among these psychic factors. Technically, such absence of being coupled is termed "dissociation." In psychiatry, for example, Bleuler's conception of schizophrenia is interpreted as "the dissolution of the personality." For analytic psychology, the degree of psychic dissociation varies with the strength of the "opposition between the conscious and the unconscious." This is what makes for the "possibility of a plurality of personalities in one and the same individual." Such a plurality is, of course, a manifestation of abnormal psychology, but the possibility for it "exists, at least potentially, within the range of normality." For the psychology of individuation it must be recognized that there is (or may be) a continuous rhythmic relation between integration and dissociation within an individual's history such that either one is "arrested" at a given stage (rejecting the contents of the on-going process) or one is able to progress, continually incorporating the manifestations of the unconscious meaningfully into "wholeness."

"The psyche not being a unity," Jung writes, "but a contradictory multiplicity of complexes, the dissociation required for our dialectics . . . is not so terribly difficult." If a state of dissociation between the individual and the collective unconscious were to be made permanent, we should have on the one hand, "the differentiated modern ego, and on the other . . . a very primitive state of affairs. We should have, in fact, what actually exists — namely, a veneer of civilization over a . . . brute. . . . But such a dissociation requires immediate synthesis and the development of what has remained undeveloped." Jung's implication is made quite clear; either there is a synthetic union of the two parts, or one of the parts, dominating consciousness, forces the other part into repression, in which case one becomes merely a characterless representation of the collective conscious life of the "civilized" or the "savage." If, on the other hand, the synthetic union of the two parts does take place, then, by "the development of what has remained undeveloped," the positive goal of individuation may be achieved. The development depends on the synthesis, and the synthesis depends on control of the libido. The control of libido depends on the symbols which unify or reconcile the dissociated elements that are in opposition.

> This is the purpose the symbol serves, and for this end it came into being, since it withdraws a certain sum of libido from the object, which is thereby relatively depreciated, bestowing the libido surplus upon the subject. But this surplus operates within the unconscious of the subject, who now finds himself between an inner and an outer determinant, whence arises the possibility of choice and a relative subjective freedom.[13]

The concept "object" is used here in the broadest possible sense, i.e., anything distinguishable from the physical or psychical reality of the subject.

> This process is . . . as old as mankind; symbols appear among the relics of prehistoric man, just as they abound among the lowest living types today. Clearly, therefore, a biological function of supreme importance must also be concerned in the symbol-forming process. Since the symbol can come to life only at

the expense of a relative depreciation of the object, it follows that its purpose is also concerned with object depreciation. If the object had an unconditional value, it would also be absolutely determining for the subject, thereby entirely prohibiting all subjective freedom of action, since even a relative freedom could no longer exist in the presence of unconditional determination by the object.

Jung points out that such relatedness to the object is tantamount to a total externalization of the process of consciousness, and such identification of subject with object (a condition found today "in attenuated form" among primitives) destroys the possibility of objective cognition. In our own thinking, the residue of this identification of object and subject is found in the phenomenon called *projection*.

Not only would such a condition prohibit cognition but it would mean a psychological inferiority in respect to feeling, as well. ". . . . Because an identity of feeling with the object possesses the following disadvantages. Firstly, any object whatsoever can affect the subject to any degree, and, secondly, any sort of affect on the part of the subject also immediately compromises and violates the object." Jung illustrates this point with the story of a bushman who had "loved" his infant son. But on the occasion of being unsuccessful at fishing, he came home in a rage, encountered his son and strangled him to death. There are manifold examples of analogous behavior, in contemporary society — on the psychological if not on the physical level of experience.

39

The word "libido" is, for Jung, "synonymous with psychic energy." There is no question here of implying an hypostasized concept of energy. "Whether or no a specific psychic force exists has nothing to do with the concept of libido." Libido is, then, used as the intensity of the psychic process—its psychological value. For our purposes here, it should now be clear that Jung is arguing in the following manner: given a certain intensity of psychic process, such energy may be disposed of in respect to the body as-an-object in relations with other body-objects (i.e., in the service of "Nature.") But some of such energy may also be disposed of by being withdrawn from its direction toward the object plane and "bestowed upon" the subject. This "quantum" of psychic energy (either in excess of what is needed to maintain the natural system, or that which is diverted from the natural system by neurotic blockages) subsequently "operates within the unconscious of the subject." Given, then, a state of tension within the individual, the possibility of choice, *a relative subjective freedom*, is created by virtue of the fact that the objects of the natural system are *not* "absolutely determining" for the subject. On the other hand, insofar as the effects of the contents of the unconscious, likewise, are *not* "absolutely determining"—the freedom of choice which the state of tension makes possible may result in the condition of dissociation rather than that of decision. The problem, now, is how free choice, either for cognitive or feeling purposes, is realized. In the terms of the psychology of individuation, this is to ask: how is integration or "wholeness" able to resolve the dissociation-tension? The answer lies in the objectification of the contents of the unconscious which have been "activated" by the quantum of psychic energy diverted to it. By such *objectification*—alone—does the psychological problem re-emerge within consciousness.

Previously, Jung had spoken of the function of symbols (in connection with the analogy of a waterpipe system for the various natural function-systems) as the "manifestation and expression" of the *excess* libido (i.e., that quantum of psychic energy which is available for withdrawal from the function-systems [It must be kept clearly in mind that this is in *contrast* to that quantum of libido which is diverted by neurotic blocks]). But now he is concerned with emphasizing the second aspect of symbols, the significance of which is that they are "transitions to new activities." In both contexts the *nature* of the symbol is the same, namely, that it expresses, as well as possible, a relatively unknown fact, which is nevertheless postulated as existing (i.e., "a complex fact not yet clearly grasped by consciousness"). But, while the nature of the symbol is defined in the same way, the *function* which a symbol performs depends on whether it operates like a siphon or like a transformer. The latter function—that operation of symbols which makes possible "transitions to new activities"—is the focus of Jung's major concern in his developed, and most elaborately expressed, theory of symbolism. This comes to be called the reconciling or unifying function, the transcendent or synthesizing function of symbols.

SECTION 4: *The Transcendent Function of Symbols*

What is available to consciousness is the *objectified* effects of the contents of the unconscious; in other words—what is available to consciousness is symbols. These manifest to consciousness the products of the process which takes place when libido has been withdrawn from the object to the subject plane. In respect to the tension which arises between the "claims" of the outer world and the "claims" of the inner world, "No adaptation can result," Jung writes, "without concessions to both worlds."[14]

> Unfortunately, our Western mind, lacking all culture in this respect, has never yet devised a concept, nor even a name, for the *union of opposites through the middle path*, that most fundamental item of inward experience, which could respectably be set against the Chinese concept of Tao. It is at once the most individual fact and the most universal, the most legitimate fulfilment of the meaning of the individual's life.

The Jungian approximation to "the middle path" is through analytic therapy. "The unconscious compensation of a neurotic conscious attitude," Jung writes, "contains all the elements that could effectively and healthily correct the one-sidedness of the conscious mind, if these elements were made conscious, i.e., understood and integrated into it as realities." This is, firstly, the goal of therapy, and secondly the scheme for the on-going condition for "wholeness" in one who has successfully incorporated the methods of the therapeutic situation into his self-regulated life, continuing beyond treatment. Understanding of the principle of *compensation*, according to Jung, is the key to both the natural process of individuation and to the methods of therapeutic treatment. In other words, the conditions for "wholeness" are implicit in the experience of dissociation. The solution requires "concessions to both worlds." Adaptation to the claims of the outer world is no more desirable, pure and simple, than adaptation to the claims of the inner world. What is desirable is that "middle path" which *reconciles* the two, so that what is achieved is not an artificial or imposed "wholeness" but such integration as is, strictly speaking, proper to the particular individual, given his particular experience of both worlds. It is for this reason that, "while the initiative lies with the unconscious . . . all criticism, choice and decision lie with the conscious mind."

Consider the function of dreams in this respect. "As a rule dreams are too feeble and too unintelligible to exercise a radical influence on consciousness. In consequence, the compensation [i.e., *the development of counterbalancing forces*] runs underground in the unconscious and has no immediate effect." Nevertheless, it does have its effect on the psyche since, if the opposition expressed by the unconscious is persistently ignored, it will result in symptoms thwarting conscious intentions. (This will readily be recognized as the pattern of "unintelligible" neurotic behavior.)

> The aim of the treatment is therefore to understand and to appreciate, so far as practicable, dreams

and all other manifestations of the unconscious, firstly in order to prevent the formation of an unconscious opposition which becomes more dangerous as time goes on, and secondly in order to make the fullest possible use of the healing factor of compensation.[15]

Insofar as dreams function according to the principle of compensation "they move along a progressive line . . . [Thus] the unconscious progressiveness and the conscious regressiveness together form a pair of opposites which, as it were, keeps the scales balanced. The influence of the educator tilts the balance in favor of progression."

Now it may be seen more clearly that the "influence of the educator" depends on *how consciousness interprets* dreams and all other manifestations of the unconscious. If the criticism or interpretation which the conscious mind makes are "right," Jung is confident, it will be "confirmed by dreams indicative of progress; in the other event correction will follow from the side of the unconscious." "The course of treatment is thus rather like a running conversation with the unconscious. . . . Just as the reward of a correct interpretation is an uprush of life, so an incorrect one dooms itself to deadlock, resistance, doubt, and mutual desiccation."

In sum, then, the interpretation of unconscious manifestations is wrong if the opposition continues; i.e., the dream, for example, which is not understood is merely an "occurrence" with ungrasped significance. Whereas, if the dream is interpreted so that its consciously appreciated significance leads to a unifying transcending of op-

44

posites (the "uprush of life" felt in the synthesis) then it becomes a living experience.

SECTION 5: *The Collective Unconscious*

All of the foregoing remarks concerning the functions of symbols, as the objectifications of the effects of the contents of the unconscious, have been expressed in terms of the analyst's discussion of therapeutic treatment, in anticipation of introducing a distinction in conceiving the unconscious which is crucial to the understanding of Jung's psychology. Manifestation of the unconscious complexes which are *signs* for the therapy of a neurosis are distinguishable from such manifestations that are *symbols*. In other words, we must differentiate between the content of signs which are *personal* and the content of unconscious effects which are genuinely symbols, i.e., *collective*.

The distinction that Jung draws between the personal and the collective unconscious stands behind the aegis of *normal* psychology. In criticizing Freud and Adler, Jung writes, "Both schools, to my way of thinking, deserve reproach for over-emphasizing the pathological aspect of life and for interpreting man too exclusively in the light of his defects. . . . For my part, I prefer to look at man in the light of what in him is healthy and sound."[16]

From the point of view of a psychology larger than that of psychopathology, Jung considers that what characterizes (all of) the unconscious for Freud and Adler — i.e., preconsciousness and subconsciousness — should be conceived as the *personal* unconscious. Preconsciousness,

45

"a term introduced by Freud, represents as it were that border zone ... which lies next to consciousness"[17] (*subliminally* perceived and felt matter). Under subconsciousness is to be understood forgotten and repressed material as well as instinctual drives. ". . . the contents of the unconscious are, according to Freud's theory, reducible to infantile tendencies and desires."[18] It is also the case that in Freud's theory the source of psychic energy (the Id) is sexual in nature and much of the contents of the unconscious are direct expressions of the Id which were conscious in infancy but have been repressed. It is precisely in respect to such content as was formerly conscious that Jung calls their unconscious manifestation *personal*. "According to this theory, the unconscious would contain only those elements of the personality which could just as well be conscious, and which have been smothered by the educational process." In respect to the "nature" of psychic energy, it would be well, at this point, to quote a passage of intellectual autobiography from Jung, in order to make clear his position.

> Freud began by taking sexuality as the only psychic driving power, and only after my break with him did he grant an equal status to other psychic activities as well. For my part, I have subsumed the various psychic drives or forces under the concept of energy in order to avoid the arbitrariness of a psychology that deals with drives or impulses alone. I therefore speak not of separate drives or forces, but of "value intensities." By what has just been said I do not mean to deny the importance of sexuality in

46

psychic life, though Freud stubbornly maintains that I do deny it. What I seek is to set bounds to the rampant terminology of sex which threatens to vitiate all discussion of the human psyche; I wish to put sexuality itself in its proper place. Common-sense will always return to the fact that sexuality is only one of the life-instincts—only one of the psycho-physiological functions—though one that is without doubt very far-reaching and important.[19]

It goes without saying that for the treatment of neurosis, the Freudian or the Adlerian psychopathology can "work." But it is Jung's position that both of those schools offer theories inadequate for normal psychology.

"The unconscious comprises not only the repressed material," Jung writes, "but also all the other psychic components which do not attain the threshold of consciousness."[20]

Insofar as it is a tenet of reductive analysis (as in Freud's or Adler's theory) that the unconscious produces no *specific* content that was not previously experienced in the conscious mind, "it ought to be possible to empty the unconscious by analysis." But, Jung argues, "besides the repressed material there are all sorts of psychic elements in the unconscious. . . . Moreover we know, from abundant experience as well as for theoretical reasons, that the unconscious must contain all the material which has *not yet* reached the threshold of consciousness." In point of fact, Jung writes, psychotherapists find that even after repressed contents have been made conscious and integrated into a patient's conscious life: "the unconscious . . .

persists no less than before in its *creative activity*."

From what has been said up to the present it follows that we should distinguish, in what is called the unconscious, a layer which we might call the *personal unconscious*.... We attribute a personal character to these elements because their effects, their partial appearance, or their origins can be rediscovered in our past.

In contradistinction to all of the manifestations of the *personal* unconscious, Jung finds, as well, a vast quantity of psychic data "having a *collective* character superordinate to the individual mentality."

Jung presents his argument by an analogy with social life.

Just as the individual is not only a separate and isolated being, but is part of society, so also the human mind is not an isolated and entirely individual fact but also a collective function. Again, even as certain social functions or tendencies are, so to speak, opposed to the egocentric interests of the individual, so also certain functions or tendencies of the human mind are opposed, by their collective nature, to the personal mental functions.

The universal similarity of human brains leads us then to admit the existence of a certain psychic function, identical with itself in all individuals; we will call it the *collective psyche*.... To borrow an expression from P. Janet, the collective psyche comprises the *parties inférieures* of the mental functions, i.e., that portion which is firmly established, is acquired by heredity, and exists everywhere; whose activity is, as it were, automatic; and which is in consequence transpersonal or impersonal. The personal conscious and unconscious comprise the *parties supérieures* of the mental functions—that is, the portion that has been ontogenetically acquired and developed, and is the result of personal differentiation.[21]

In the chapter devoted to definition of his terms in Jung's *Psychological Types,* the idea of the collective unconscious is expressed as such contents as "do not originate in personal acquisitions but in the inherited possibility of psychic functioning in general, namely, in the inherited brain-structure. These are the mythological associations —those motives and images which can spring anew in every age and clime, without historical tradition or migration. I term these contents the *collective unconscious.* Just as conscious contents are engaged in a defiinite activity, the unconscious contents—so experience teaches us—are similarly active. Just as certain results or products proceed from conscious psychic activity, there are also products of unconscious activity, as for instance dreams and phantasies."[22]

However clear Jung has tried to make his formulation of the *collective* unconscious, it has frequently been *misinterpreted* to mean that *ideas are inherited.* Even in one of his earliest formulations, in the *Psychological Types,* written in 1920, a typical statement concerning the introduction of the idea of the collective unconscious reads:

49

> Since earliest times, the inborn manner of *acting* has been called *instinct*, and for this manner of psychic apprehension of the object I have proposed the term *archetype*. . . . This term embraces the same idea as contained in "primordial image" (an expression borrowed from Jakob Burckhardt) . . .

That is to say, just as the word "instinct" names the idea of an inborn *manner* of acting, not particular actions, so the word "archetype" names the idea of an inborn *manner* of apprehending, feeling, intuiting or thinking, not particular perceptions, feelings, intuitions or thoughts.

Nevertheless, as late as in his essay "The Spirit of Psychology," written in 1946, one finds Jung defending his position on this point against the same misconstruction.

> What above all stultifies understanding is the arrant assumption that "archetype" means an inborn idea. . . . Archetypes are typical *forms* of behavior which, once they become conscious, naturally present themselves as ideas and images, like everything else that becomes a content of consciousness.[23]

For purposes of scholarship, it would be well to follow something of the historical development of Jung's expression of the idea through his major writings. The concept of the collective unconscious was first introduced in his book in 1912 (entitled *The Psychology of the Unconscious*, in its first English translation, but which has been revised for the Collected Edition of his works and now appears under a title closer to the original German: *Symbols of Transformation*. The subtitle of the work is

"An Analysis of the Prelude to a Case of Schizophrenia").

In the course of attempting to understand the significance of a series of dreams of a "small business employee with no more than a secondary school education,"[24] Jung was confronted with material in symbolic form which (it later proved) showed an extremely high degree of similarity to ancient and remote cultural expressions. The patient could not possibly have had previous conscious knowledge of them; there was no possibility of this being a case of cryptomnesia. Nor was there the possibility of "suggestion" from the analyst, since Jung himself did not learn of the antique cultural parallel until four years later.

The problem of explaining the parallels subsequently presented itself to him in the following manner:

> ... it is a controversial point whether the inner images, or collective representations, are merely suggested by the environment, or whether they are genuine and spontaneous experiences. The first view simply begs the question, because it is obvious that the content suggested must have come into existence somehow and at some time. There was a time when the utterances of mythology were entirely original, when they were numinous experiences, and anyone who takes the trouble can observe these subjective experiences even today.

It is on the basis of numerous similar analytic experiences that Jung, then, *inferred*—for his general psychology—the spontaneous source of images of which an individual had had no previous conscious knowledge, i.e., inferred the existence of the collective unconscious.

This observation was not an isolated case: it was manifestly not a question of inherited ideas, but of an inborn disposition to produce parallel images, or rather identical psychic structures common to all men, which I later called the archetypes of the collective unconscious. They correspond to the concept of the "pattern of behavior" in biology.

[The *collective* unconscious] ... is universal: it not only binds individuals together into a nation or race, but unites them with the men of the past and with their psychology. Thus, by reason of its supra-individual universality, the unconscious is the prime object of any real psychology that claims to be more than psychophysics.

Thus, in *Symbols of Transformation*, Jung announced his break with Freud's theory of psychology and laid the groundwork for rectifying what he considered the imbalance of reductive analysis by its emphasis on the pathological and its limitation for interpretation of spiritual activities—namely, art, religion, and science—to that of "substitute gratification" for the frustrations of the sexual libido.

Jung's next major book, *Two Essays on Analytical Psychology*, was written during 1916; and like the so-called *Psychology of the Unconscious*, underwent frequent and extensive revisions. In this work he presents the following propositions.

Through the act of cognition we "posit" the

reality of the archetypes, or, more precisely, we postulate the psychic existence of such contents on a cognitive basis. It must emphatically be stated that it is not just a question of cognitive contents, but of transubjective, largely autonomous, psychic systems which on that account are only very conditionally under the control of the conscious mind and for the most part escape it altogether.[25]

For the conscious elaboration of this material the transcendent function reveals itself as a mode of apprehension mediated by the archetypes and capable of uniting the opposites. . . . A general account of this process, which may extend over a long period of time, would be pointless — even if such a description were possible — because it takes the greatest imaginable variety of forms in different individuals. The only common factor is the emergence of certain definite archetypes. I would mention in particular the shadow, the animal, the wise old man, the anima, the animus, . . . besides an indefinite number of archetypes representative of situations. A special position must be accorded to those archetypes which stand for the goal of the developmental process. . . . The meaning and purpose of the process is the realization, in all its aspects, of the personality originally hidden away in the embryonic germ-plasm; the production and unfolding of the original, potential wholeness. . . . For these reasons I have termed this the *individuation process.*

In Jung's *Two Essays* the function of symbols as the

means for the "middle way," i.e., the mediating principle between consciousness and the archetypes of the collective unconscious, is more elaborately considered — with particular reference to *religion* (as one of the symbolic systems effective in this respect).

> [The energy of the archetypes which have been activated] ... becomes serviceable again by being brought into play through man's conscious attitude toward the collective unconscious. The religions have established this cycle of energy in a concrete way by means of ritual communion with the gods.

Earlier, in *Symbols of Transformation*, Jung had suggested that "Christ, as a hero and god-man, signifies psychologically the self; that is, he represents the projection of this most important and most central of archetypes. The archetype of the self has, functionally, the significance of a ruler of the inner world, i.e., of the collective unconscious."[26] (This suggestion of 1912 was taken up again in 1951 and examined at length in Jung's volume *Aion: Contributions to the Symbolism of the Self*.) But here in the *Two Essays*, Jung defends the early insight with the argument:

> It is after all only a tiny fraction of humanity, living mainly on that thickly populated peninsula of Asia which juts out into the Atlantic Ocean, and calling themselves "cultured," who, because they lack all contact with nature, have hit upon the idea that religion is a peculiar kind of mental disturbance of undiscoverable purport. Viewed from a safe dis-

tance, say from central Africa or Tibet, it would certainly look as if this fraction had projected its own unconscious mental derangements upon nations still possessed of healthy instincts.

Art and science, as well as religion, come to be considered, at length, subsequently, as significant symbolic systems—in the service of Spirit or Culture; systems whose symbolic purport is discoverable in relation with the archetypes of the collective unconscious.

In *Psychological Types*, published in 1920, Jung makes numerous important additions to his psychology (here primarily in respect to the psychology of consciousness) which places it, for our purposes, halfway between the development of his interpretation of religion and that of art. A great deal of the material he employs here, as illustrative of his interpretative principles, is concerned with art in the service of religion. In respect to the withdrawal of psychic energy from the object plane to that of the subject, Jung writes:

> The archetype is a symbolic formula, which always begins to function whenever there are no conscious ideas present, or when such as are present are impossible upon intrinsic or extrinsic grounds. The contents of the collective unconscious are represented in consciousness in the form of pronounced tendencies, or definite ways of looking at things. They are generally regarded by the individual as being determined by the object—incorrectly, at bottom—since they have their source in the unconscious structure of the psyche, and are only released

by the operation of the object. These subjective tendencies and ideas are stronger than the objective influence; because their psychic value is higher, they are imposed upon all impressions.[27]

As a result of introducing the concept of the collective unconsciousness, it is now possible to understand much more accurately what was meant earlier by saying that study of the objectifications of the effects of the contents of the unconscious is crucial for the formulation of Jung's theory of symbolism. What had been implied, and may now be made explicit, was that symbols—properly so called—are the (objectified) effects of the archetypes of the *collective* unconscious, activated by the psychic energy diverted from or in excess to the natural-functions systems. Concerning the difference between *signs* of neurotic malfunctions (i.e., symptoms of the *personal* unconscious in a reductive psychoanalysis) and *symbols* of the archetypes of the collective unconscious, Jung writes in *Psychological Types:*

> There are, of course, neurotics who regard their unconscious products, which are primarily symptoms, as symbols of supreme importance. Generally, however, this is not the case. On the contrary, the neurotic of to-day is only too prone to regard a product that may actually be full of significance, as a "symptom."

In the Conclusion of *Psychological Types,* Jung writes, "In order to discover the *uniformity* of the human psyche I must descend into the very foundations of consciousness. *Only there* do I find wherein all are alike."

> ... I have embraced [this uniformity] in the con-
> cept of the collective unconscious, as a universal and
> homogeneous substratum whose homogeneity ex-
> tends into a world-wide identity or similarity of
> myths and fairy tales; so that a negro of the Southern
> States of America dreams in the motives of Grecian
> mythology, and a Swiss grocer's apprentice repeats
> in his psychosis, the vision of an Egyptian Gnostic.

"But," he adds, "if I wish to develop the picture of the
psyche in its *completeness*, I must keep in mind the fact
of the *diversity* of psyches, since the *conscious individual
psyche* belongs just as much to the general picture of
psychology as does its unconscious foundation."

> What immeasurable distances lie between the con-
> sciousness of a primitive, a Themistoclean Athenian,
> and a modern European! What a difference between
> the consciousness of the learned professor and that of
> his spouse! !

But to return to the theme of the development and
exposition of the concept, *collective unconscious*, in
Jung's writings. Just as he had introduced the idea of the
"engram" in the *Two Essays*, where he wrote:

> ... the contents of the collective unconscious are
> not only the residues of archaic, specifically human
> modes of functioning, but also the residues of func-
> tions from man's animal ancestry, whose duration
> in time was infinitely greater than the relatively brief

epoch of specifically human existence. These residues, or "engrams," as Semon calls them, etc.

so Jung continues to use the term in *Psychological Types*, to add to his idea of the archetypes or primordial images of the collective unconscious.

> The primordial image is a mnemic deposit, an *imprint* ("engram"—Semon) which has arisen through the condensation of innumerable, similar processes. It is primarily a precipitate or deposit, and therefore a typical basic form of a certain ever-recurring psychic experience. As a mythological motive, therefore, it is a constantly effective and continually recurring expression which is either awakened, or appropriately formulated, by certain psychic experiences.[28]

In an essay written in 1922, which became a chapter of the volume *Contributions to Analytical Psychology* (published in English first in 1928) Jung remarks:

> In itself the collective unconscious cannot be said to exist at all; that is to say, it is nothing but a possibility, that possibility in fact which from primordial time has been handed down to us in the defiinite form of mnemic images, or expressed in anatomical formations in the very structure of the brain. It does not yield innate ideas, but inborn possibilities of ideas, which also set definite bounds to the most daring phantasy.[29]

That is, the "ontological" nature of the collective un-

SECTION 5: *The Collective Unconscious*

conscious is not known. What the collective unconscious
is said to perform is, however, the work of making available the conditions for imaginative thought. Such "conditions" would be comparable to Kant's conception of
a priori "Ideas" of thought, or Schopenhauer's conception
of (Platonic) forms. The various more-or-less specific
(Kantian) "Ideas" are the archetypes; and here Jung ex-
pands metaphorically on these images to clarify the function of the archetype.

> [Each] is like a deeply graven river-bed in the soul,
> in which the waters of life, that had spread hitherto
> with groping and uncertain course over wide but
> shallow surfaces, suddenly become a mighty river.

This is why the most powerful contributions to the
development of spiritual life—in religion, art, and science
— have the effective powers they possess, namely, "the
most effective ideals are always more or less transparent
variants of the archetype."

> The individual man is never able to use his powers
> to their fullest range, unless there comes to his aid
> one of those collective presentations we call ideals
> that liberates in his soul all the hidden forces of in-
> stinct, to which the ordinary conscious will alone
> can never gain access.

As Jung's research and interpretations proceed historically, he is concerned with testing his hypothesis by applying it to the histories of religion, art, and scientific
thought, in order to discover whether the implications he
has drawn can be substantiated. In respect to each of these

59

fields of cultural activity, his point of reference is the same: the functional analysis of the process of individuation. Obviously, he argues, the objectifications of the archetypes — in religion, art, and science —"are no longer contents of the unconscious, but have already changed into conscious formulas." [30]

There is considerable difference between such an archetype and the formula that has become historic or has been elaborated. Especially on the higher levels of esoteric teaching, the archetypes appear in a form that usually reveals in an unmistakable way the elements of judgement and valuation introduced by conscious elaboration. On the other hand, their immediate manifestation, as it confronts us in dreams and visions, is much more natural, less understandable or more naive than in the myth, for example. In this respect the fairy tale is, no doubt, much truer to nature.

Nevertheless, he points out, even in the analyses of fairy tale and myth, "we have almost completely refused to see that [they] are first and foremost psychic manifestations that represent the nature of the psyche." In the 1940's and 50's, Jung carried out precisely such interpretations in his volumes *Essays on a Science of Mythology*, *Psychology and Religion: West and East*, and in *Psychology and Alchemy*, as well as in his contribution to *The Interpretation of Nature and the Psyche*.

Through them all he remains true to his primary intuitions. In *Essays On a Science of Mythology* (1940) he writes, "The methodological principle in accordance with which psychology treats the products of the unconscious is this: Contents of an archetypal character are manifestations of processes in the collective unconscious. Hence they do not refer to anything that is or has been conscious, but to something essentially unconscious. In the last analysis, therefore, *it is impossible to say what they refer to.*"[31]

> ... all we can do is to circumscribe and give an approximate description of an *unconscious core of meaning.* The ultimate meaning of this nucleus was never conscious and never will be ...
>
> What an archetypal content is always expressing is first and foremost a *figure of speech.* (Every interpretation necessarily remains an "as-if.")
>
> If it speaks of the sun and identifies with it the lion, the king, the hoard of gold guarded by the dragon, or the force that makes for the life and health of man, it is neither the one thing nor the other, but the unknown third thing that finds more or less adequate expression in all these similes, yet — to the perpetual vexation of the intellect — remains unknown and not to be fitted into a formula.

And lastly, he states, in a passage which not only summarizes this conception of the contents of the collective unconscious but, also, initiates remarks concerning their non-reductive, "synthetic," analysis:

> Not for a moment dare we succumb to the illusion that an archetype can be finally explained and disposed of. Even the best attempts at explanation are

only more or less successful translations into another metaphorical language. (Indeed, language itself is only a metaphor.) The most we can do is to *dream the myth onwards* and give it a modern dress.

Here, then, the archetypes are conceived not only as residual riverbeds which make possible the most intense channeling of psychic energy, but as "organs" of the psyche for which there is no rational substitute. That is to say, if we interpret their manifestations wrongly, we have misunderstood the demands of an organic function, from which only psychic distress can follow. In effect, it must be understood that the archetypes are by no means merely passive conduits of psychic energy but active agents, as well. They are agents operating in a compensatory way to the end of bringing about a state of health for the individual psyche.

> [The archetypes] is an [independent] organism, "endowed with creative force"; for the primordial image is an inherited organization of psychic energy, a rooted system, which is not only an expression of the energic process but also a possibility for its operation. In a sense, it characterizes the way in which the energic process from earliest time has always run its unvarying course, while at the same time enabling a perpetual repetition of the law-determined course to take place; since it provides just that character of apprehension or psychic grasp of situations which continually yield a further continuation of life. It is, therefore, the necessary counterpart of *instinct*, which is an appropriate form of action also presup-

posing a grasp of the momentary situation that is both purposeful and suitable. This apprehension of the given situation is vouchsafed by the a priori existing image. It represents the practicable formula without which the apprehension of a new state of affairs would be impossible.[32]

When science studies physical organs, it examines them anatomically, histologically, and embryologically. But the *meaning* of an organ is arrived at only when studied teleologically, i.e., in answer to the question: what is its biological purpose? This is the question which physiology answers in terms of the well-being of the body as a whole. Likewise, Jung argues, it is the business of psychology to ask and answer the teleological question: what is the purpose of the archetypes? The answer is formulated in respect to the process of individuation. Subsequently, the principle may be extended to the life of mankind, and the symbolic systems of religion, art, and science can, therefore, be interpreted in respect to the psychological significance.

Now, having examined the development of Jung's distinctive thinking about the unconscious, it will be possible to return to our major concern—his theory of symbolism—equipped to understand his interpretation more adequately.

SECTION 6: *The Conditions of Symbolic Interpretation*

I. "HERMENEUTICS"

The summary statement has already been made explicit: namely, that symbols are the objectified effects of the archetypes of the collective unconscious. Thus, the principles which Jung's psychology contributes to the fields of cultural history can make possible a psychological account of the meaningfulness of symbolic systems, e.g., art, religion, and science, rather than a psychological method which would "explain away" such activities as "substitute gratifications."

In its nature, then, the symbol expresses in the best possible description or formula, a relatively unknown fact, which is nevertheless experienced as existing. Were the referent of such an expression clearly know*able* or known, the description or formula would not be a symbol but a sign. "A view which interprets the symbolic expression as an intentional transcription or transformation of a known thing is allegoric." [33]

The reason that the referents of symbols, properly so-called, are *relatively unknown* is that — while it is possible to speak of such referents as a class, The Archetyes of the Collective Unconscious, and to specify *to some degree* distinguishable "characters" among them — it is a delusion, Jung warns, to pretend that one can "explain" what they are.

Given the nature of symbols conceived in these terms, Jung distinguishes between the functions of symbols: namely, those used for the purpose of withdrawing psychic energy from the natural-functions system and those used for the purpose of transforming such diverted or excess energy to the service of spirit or culture. In this latter respect, symbols make possible "transitions to new activities." They do so by serving the purpose of synthesizing or unifying factors between consciousness and the unconscious which, previously in a state of conflict (at the worst: dissociation), are reconciled and transcended. In the psychic economy of the individual within whom such a private transcending symbol emerges, his personal process of individuation can be said to progress; in the cultural economy of the group to which he belongs, the publicly objectified effects of that personal progressive development may be said to function in such ways as both "lead men to premonition while defending them against experience."[34] What enables one person to become more properly himself, likewise, enables his group to further meaningful possibilities within its cultural life.

> [The symbol] attemps to elucidate, by means of analogy, something that still belongs entirely to the domain of the unknown or something that is yet to be. Imagination reveals to us, in the form of a more or less striking analogy, what is in process of becoming. If we reduce this by analysis to something else universally known, we destroy the authentic value of the symbol; but to attribute hermeneutic significance to it conforms to its value and its meaning.[35]

What Jung implies by comparing this aspect of an analytic-therapy practice with the "science" of hermeneutics had been foreshadowed, in another context, with the phrase: "The most we can do is to *dream the myth onwards* and give it a modern dress."[36] Hermeneutics, "which was widely practised in former times, consists in making successive additions of other analogies to the analogy given in the symbol."[37] In therapy, Jung describes the procedure of considering, first of all, the subjective analogies which the patient produces at random in trying to "dream the myth onwards." Secondly, the analyst and patient together consider the objective analogies found in the course of research in various cultural fields.

This procedure widens and enriches the initial symbol, and the final outcome is an infinitely complex and varied picture, in which certain "lines" of psychological development stand out as possibilities that are at once individual and collective. There is no science on earth by which these lines could be proved "right": on the contrary, rationalism could very easily prove that they are not right. Their validity is proved by their intense value for life. And that is what matters from the point of view of practical treatment. . . . Hermeneutic treatment of imaginative ideas leads to the synthesis of the individual and the collective psyche. [The intervening passage refers to the difficulties encountered in practice when the patient refuses to take himself seriously, and to cooperate with the "advice" of his own unconscious; after which Jung concludes:] . . . As soon as ever we begin to map out the lines of advance that are symbolically indicated, the patient must begin to proceed along them. If he remains hypocritically inert, his own inaction precludes any cure. He is in truth obliged to take the way of individual life which is revealed to him, and to persist in it until and unless an unmistakable reaction from his unconscious warns him that he is on the wrong track.

66

II. RELATIVITY OF SYMBOLIC VALUES

In respect to the (regressive) attitude of refusal to take seriously such discoveries (as conscious criticism and interpretation make) of "lines" for development derived from unconscious content—proper to the individual patient—it would be appropriate to consider Jung's remarks concerning the *relativity* of the symbol in general.

> Whether a thing is a symbol or not depends chiefly upon the attitude of the consciousness considering it; as for instance, a mind that regards the given facts not merely as such but also as an expression of the yet unknown.
>
> ... every psychological phenomenon is a symbol when we are willing to assume that it purports, or signifies, something different and still greater, something therefore which is withheld from present knowledge.

Such an attitude—a disposition, a willingness—to be open to the possibility of a symbol may be said to be common among persons who have had the aesthetic experience of such expressions as "mean more than they say." In his examination of the relativity of symbols, Jung's interpretation of meaning has this in common with the Pragmatic and Existential interpretations: that meaningfulness is dependent upon the attitude of the interpreting consciousness. In effect, the attitude which makes the appreciation of a symbol possible is a conscious concern in the service of meaning as contrasted to consciousness in the service of facts.

> This view [the symbolic attitude] ... stands op-

67

posed to another view, which lays the accent upon pure actuality, and subordinates meaning to facts. For this latter view there can be no symbol at all, wherever the symbolism depends exclusively upon the manner of consideration.

Nevertheless, Jung takes the existence of the contrast between these two views of things (which are mutually contradictory) as evidence for the theory that there are objective differences between processes which express no particular meaning (i.e., have no intrinsic meaning) but are merely consequences or *symptoms*, and, on the other hand, processes "which bear within them a hidden meaning, processes which have not merely arisen from something, but also tend to become something, and are therefore *symbols*."[38]

> It is left to our judgment and criticism to decide whether the thing we are dealing with is a symptom or a symbol.

The decision which is made that an expression *is* a symbol may have either individual or social significance. "There are individual psychic products, whose manifest symbolic character at once compels a symbolic conception. . . . Such products, however, never have an exclusive conscious or unconscious source, but proceed from a uniform cooperation of both. Purely conscious products are no more convincingly symbolic, per se, than purely unconscious products, and vice versa; it devolves, therefore, upon the symbolical attitude of the observing consciousness to endow them with the character of a symbol.

But they may equally well be conceived as mere causally conditioned facts, in much the same sense as one might regard the red exanthema of scarlet fever as a 'symbol' of the disease." In connection with this point, it would be well to refer to the previous remark to the effect that, generally speaking, the neurotic of today is only too prone to regard a product that may be full of significance (indicating a "line" for his future development) as merely a symptom expressive of a condition rooted in the past.

> The living symbol shapes and formulates an essential unconscious factor, and the more generally this factor prevails, the more general is the operation of the symbol; for in every soul it touches an associated chord.

That is to say, for an expression to become a symbol of social as well as individual significance it must be the best possible expression of something still uknown (for a given cultural time-place) — which proceeds from a highly complex (individual) mental atmosphere; at the same time it must "embrace and contain that which relates to a considerable *group* of men for such an effect to be within its power, it must contain just that which may be common to a large group of men . . . it must be something that is still so primitive that its omnipresence stands beyond all doubt. Only when the symbol comprises this something, and brings it to its highest possible expression, has it any general efficacy. Therein consists the potent and at the same time, redeeming effect of a living, social symbol."

Obviously, Jung's use of the word "living" in this connection is metaphoric, and he develops the metaphor con-

69

sciously. A symbol, he says, is *alive* "only in so far as it is pregnant with meaning. But, if its meaning is born out of it," if it is formulated so explicitly as to express the implicit meaning exhaustively, "then the symbol is *dead*, i.e., it possesses only a historical significance."

> For every esoteric explanation the symbol is dead, since through esoterism it has been brought to a better expression (at least ostensibly), whereupon it merely serves as a conventional sign for associations which are more completely and better known elsewhere. Only for the exoteric standpoint is the symbol always living.

III. RATIONALITY OR IRRATIONALITY OF SYMBOLS

The question of whether a symbol should be thought of as rational or irrational is answered somewhat contradictorily by Jung. In one of the beginning sections of *Psychological Types*, where he discusses the Chinese (Taoistic religious) symbol of Yin and Yang, and again when discussing the idea of the Messiah in Judaism and Christianity, Jung speaks of such symbols simply as irrational.

> Reason must always seek the solution (of conflicts) upon rational, sequential, logical ways, in which it is certainly justified in all normal situations; but in the greatest and really decisive questions the reason proves inadequate. It is incapable of creating the image, the symbol; for the symbol is irrational.

However, in the concluding section of that volume, devoted to definitions, Jung writes of this question with a more complex answer. Because a symbol is the product of a complex nature, which proceeds from *every* psychic function's contribution to it: "it is neither rational nor irrational." In respect to these psychic modes which Jung stipulates as the four basis ones, namely, thinking, feeling, intuiting and sensing, he writes:

> [The symbol] certainly has one side that accords with reason, but it has also another side that is inaccessible to reason; for not only the data of reason, but also the irrational data of pure inner and outer perception, have entered into its nature. The prospective meaning and pregnant significance of the symbol appeals just as strongly to thinking as to feeling, while its peculiar plastic imagery when shaped into senuous form stimulates sensation as much as intuition.

The living symbol, therefore, cannot be created by a dull or undeveloped mind, "for such a man will rest content with the already existing symbols offered by established tradition." For the lively and developed mind, "for whom the dictated symbol no longer contains the highest reconciliation in one expression," the passionate yearning for a better formulation, makes the creation of a new symbol possible.

It must be recognized that a living symbol cannot be manufactured. A formulation that is pregnant with genuine significance and functions as a reconciling factor cannot be produced by consciousness alone; the result of such an attempt would contain nothing beyond what was put into it — i.e., what was previously known. Yearning for a better formulation is not enough.

But, inasmuch as the symbol proceeds from his highest and latest mental achievement and must also include the deepest roots of his being, it cannot be a onesided product of the most highly differentiated mental functions, but must at least have an equal source, in the lowest and most primitive motions of his psyche. For this cooperation of antithetic states to be at all possible, they must stand side by side in fullest conscious opposition.

This condition of disunion within oneself — with the ego recognizing and participating in both — is the situation previously described as dissociation. Should the dissociation be resolved by the subordination of one part, the confrontation of opposites will not result in a symbol but, rather, in a symptom of the repressed antithesis, i.e., it will be disproportionately the product of the repressed element. And "to the extent in which a symbol is merely a symptom, it also lacks the redeeming effect, since it fails to express the full right to existence of every portion of the psyche, constantly calling to mind the suppression of the antithesis, although consciousness may omit to take this into account."

The redeeming, synthesizing, transcending power of a genuine symbol depends on the recognized equality of the factors in opposition. The development of a symbol can, therefore, be described in the following way: when the ego recognizes the equal rights of the opposed conscious and unconscious factors, there results a suspension of will. This condition of dissociation is constituted by the tension of opposites which arises out of the damming up of libido behind each of the factors. Under these circumstances, "since life cannot tolerate suspension . . . the inactivity of the conscious brings about an activity of the unconscious. . . ."

> Through the activity of the unconscious, a content is unearthed which is constellated by thesis and antithesis in equal measure, and is related to both in a compensatory relation. Since this content discloses a relation to both thesis and antithesis, it forms a middle territory, upon which the opposites can be reconciled.

The more effective the symbol, then, the more "primitive" its source in the collective unconscious. Such content as is "unearthed" through this activity in the unconscious reflects in consciousness something of the infinitely variable archetypes. That it is "constellated"—assembled into a unit, a fixed group of interrelated parts — refers not only to the content contributed by the factors of which consciousness is cognizant in the tension of opposites, but also to the form given it by the activity of the collective unconscious. Such a constellation characterizes the middle way: the condition for transcendence that makes possible progress beyond the stage of internal conflict. Without such a means for reconciliation no progress is possible; only various delaying actions of a regressive and repressive — neurotic — nature.

If, for example, the conflict is between sensuality and spirituality: ". . . spirituality tries to make something spiritual out of the unconscious expression, while sensuality

73

aims at something sensual; the one wishing to create science and art from the new expression, the other sensual experience." If the ego makes its investment with one of these principles to the detriment of the other, the conflict, although temporarily resolved, continues "in a subsequent repetition of the process of division upon a higher plane."

> But if, through the resoluteness of the ego, neither thesis nor antithesis can succeed in resolving the unconscious product, this is sufficient demonstration that the unconscious expression is superior to both sides.

Now we have clearly before us all of the terms required for Jung's theory of symbolism. What the unconscious contributes, through being activated by the libido diverted to it in the condition of suspension of will — during which the ego entertains the tension of opposites evaluated as having equal psychic claims — is the *form* of a mediatory expression. The raw material, the content to be formed, is elaborated in the thesis and antithesis which are in opposition. The "steadfastness of the ego," in its refusal to make an either/or choice between the opposites, is "mutually conditioning" with the transcending function itself in order that a living symbol might arise.

> It would appear at times as though the fixity of the inborn individuality were the decisive factor, at times as though the mediatory expression possessed a superior force prompting the ego to absolute steadfastness. But, in reality, it is quite conceivable that

74

the firmness and certainty of the individuality on the one hand, and the superior force of the mediatory product on the other, are merely tokens of one and the same fact. When the mediatory product is preserved in this way, it fashions a raw product which is for construction, not for dissolution, and which becomes a common object for both thesis and antithesis; thus it becomes a new content that governs the whole attitude, putting an end to the division, and forcing the energy of the opposites into a common channel. The suspension of life is, therewith, abolished, and the individual life can compass a greater range with new energy and new goals.[39]

One may now see all of the elements at play in the production of a symbol. For an expression to serve this function it must not be exclusively the product of either the consciousness or the unconscious. What the unconscious activity contributes is the archetypal forms by which the content of consciously experienced conflict may be synthesized. But whether such formulations are interpreted adequately for the reconciliation of opposites to take place effectively depends on the attitude of the conscious mind that must interpret and criticize. It is in this sense that the symbol is both irrational and rational.

IV. EXAMPLES OF SYMBOLIC INTERPRETATION

In the light of this analysis, it is possible now to see what Jung means by the *prospective significance* of a symbol. Speaking in general of the role of archetypes, or speaking abstractly of their "characters," is never as clear as considering how, in any concrete instance, they contribute to the formulation of a synthesis. Interpreted by the "steadfast" ego in respect to lines for development, the most important aspect of the symbol is the quality of futurity — the indication of what *ought to become.*

> In the essential rawness of its material . . . lies its prospective significance, and in the form which its crude material receives through the influence of the opposites, lies its effective power over all the psychic functions.

"In the form . . . lies its effective power." This is the crucial concept for understanding Jung's theory of symbolism. Clearly, this is diametrically opposed to those interpretations of psychic manifestations for which "content" is all, and form contributes nothing to knowledge. In the conflict between the attitude for which all meaning is invested in actuality or "fact" and the symbolical attitude, the value of Jung's position lies in its emphasizing the meaningfulness of such expressions interpreted as having prospective significance. On the purely pragmatic principle of effectiveness, depending upon whether a psychic formulation "turns out" to have pointed the right way for future usefulness or not, the value of an expression or formulation qua *symbol* is defended. It is the *form* of the expression which makes possible the reconciling function of a symbol; and herein lies the key by which Jung's psychology of individuation can enter into discussions of religion, science, and *art.*

(a) *From Physical Science.* To take an example from the field of physical science, in his *Two Essays on Analyt-*

ical Psychology, Jung considers the origin of "one of the greatest thoughts which the nineteenth century brought to birth: the idea of the conservation of energy."

Robert Mayer, who presented the idea, was not a physicist but a medical doctor. For the year 1840-41, Mayer sailed in the Far East as a ship's doctor. During this period he made a number of physiological investigations. He wrote, in a letter quoted by Jung, of how "if one wants to be clear on matters of physiology, some knowledge of physical processes is essential," and, therefore, working at physical problems in his cabin while the ship docked at romantic Oriental ports. ". . . I passed many an hour as though *inspired*, the like of which I cannot remember either before or since. Some flashes of thought that passed through me while in the roads of Surabaya were at once assiduously followed up, and in their turn led to fresh subjects. Those times have passed, but the quiet examination of that which then came to the surface in me has taught me that it is a truth, which cannot only be subjectively felt, but objectively proved."[40]

Jung remarks on the origin of the idea of the conservation of energy ". . . it is very important to realize that the idea was not, strictly speaking, 'made' by Mayer. Nor did it come into being through the fusion of ideas or scientific hypotheses then extant, but grew in its creator like a plant." Jung quotes from G. F. Helm's book on energetics: "Robert Mayer's new idea did not detach itself gradually from the traditional concepts of energy by deeper reflection on them, but belongs to those intuitively apprehended ideas which, arising in other realms of a spiritual nature, as it were take possession of the mind and

77

compel it to reshape the traditional conceptions in their own likeness."

Jung then poses the question: "Whence this new idea that thrusts itself upon consciousness with such elemental force? And whence did it derive the power that could so seize upon consciousness that it completely eclipsed the multitudinous impressions of a first voyage to the tropics?" He posits, then, ". . . if we apply our theory here, the explanation can only be this: *the idea of energy and its conservation must be a primordial image that was dormant in the collective unconscious.*"[41]

In order to maintain the interpretation, Jung is obliged to "prove that a primordial image of this kind really did exist in the mental history of mankind and was operative through the ages."

> As a matter of fact, this proof can be produced without much difficulty: the most primitive religions in the most widely separated parts of the earth are founded upon this image. These are the so-called dynamistic religions whose sole and determining thought is that there exists a universal magical power about which everything revolves. Tylor, the well-known English investigator, and Frazer likewise, misunderstood this idea as animism. In reality primitives do not mean, by their power-concept, souls or spirits at all, but something which the American investigator Lovejoy has appropriately termed "primitive energetics."

Jung then traces the connection of this idea with concepts of soul, spirit, God, health, bodily strength, fertility, magic, prestige, and medicine as well as with certain states of feeling — particularly among the Polynesians, in the Old Testament, in the Gospels, in Heraclitus, among the Persians, and the Stoics; "and in the Buddhist and primitive notion of metempsychosis — transmigration of souls — is implicit its unlimited changeability together with its constant preservation."

> So the idea has been stamped on the human brain for aeons. That is why it lies ready to hand in the unconscious of every man. Only, certain conditions are needed to cause it to appear. These conditions were evidently fulfilled in the case of Robert Mayer. The greatest and best thoughts of man shape themselves upon these primordial images as upon a blueprint.

A theoretical idea such as the conservation of energy may be thought of as a reconciling, synthesizing, transcending "symbol"—"inasmuch as every scientific theory contains a hypothesis, and therefore an anticipatory designation of a fact still essentially unknown, it is a symbol."[42] Its function of transcendence and reconciliation is attested to by virtue of its ability to explain otherwise dissociated "laws" within the field, and its synthesizing function likewise makes possible the development of further laws and hypotheses.

This may seem to be a rather far fetched possibility for explaining the origin of scientific theories, but one can only humbly recognize that there is no generally accepted psychology of rational thought, and that Jung offers here indication of a line for such research which

79

may prove to be of value despite its apparent difficulties at first.

(It should be noted before proceeding to the example of symbolic interpretation of a work of religious literature that these two examples are by no means representative of the quantity of such studies by Jung. Here, one example of each is presented. But the example from the physical sciences is the *only* one of such a nature that I have found in Jung's writings; the example from religious literature is one among dozens of such a kind.)

(b) *From Religious Literature*. To take an example of Jung's investigations into the origins of symbolic forms from the field of religion is to choose from what is now a great wealth of material. For the sake of brevity, one may consider at this point his examination of the symbolism in a volume of Early Christian writing, *The Shepherd* of Hermas, written in Greek about 140 A.D. The book consists of a number of visions and revelations, which, Jung judges: "symbolically represent the consolidation of the new faith."[43]

Of symbols which reconcile opposites, Jung writes, the *service of God* is the Christian principle; in Buddhism it is *service of the self* (self-development); in Goethe's doctrines it is *service of the soul*, symbolized by the *service of woman*. Referring to the formulation by Goethe, Jung writes:

> Contained herein is the principle of modern individualism on the one hand, and on the other a primitive polydaemonism which assigns, not merely to every race but to every tribe, every family, even to

every individual, its own religious principle. . . . Individualism seems to have begun with the service of woman . . .

Tracing this representation of the psychological interpretation backward in time from Goethe through medieval material, to Dante and the Litany of Loretto, Jung arrives at Hermas' *The Shepherd*, which offers "in a most concise and comprehensive form . . . this characteristic transition from the service of woman to the service of the soul."

It is the story of a Greek slave who had been in the service of a Roman woman named Rhoda, who gave him his freedom. He had become a Christian, married and raised a family, before he encountered Rhoda again, in later years. He sees her bathing in the Tiber and helps her out of the river. Jung writes, ". . . probably as much from gratitude as from pleasure, a feeling of love was stirred in his heart; which, however, so far as he was aware, had merely the character of brotherly love." Nevertheless, "this was the starting-point for the visionary episode that followed."

Hermas' erotic wish for possession of Rhoda becomes conscious; but on the basis of his Christian prohibitions the desire is repressed. ". . . this repressed libido evoked a powerful transformation in his unconscious, for it imbued the soul image with life, thus bringing it to spontaneous efficacy." What is meant here by the phrase "the soul image" will become clear subsequently.

Shortly afterward, Hermas relates, while making a trip to Cumae, he fell asleep and experienced a vision in

81

which Rhoda appeared to him and announced that she had "charged thee with thy sins before the Lord." Hermas remonstrates that he has never spoken an evil word to her, nor thought of her but as a sister, if not a goddess; but she responds with the chastisement that " 'The desire of sin arose in thy heart. Or is it not indeed a sin in thine eyes for a just man to cherish a sinful desire in his heart? Verily, it is a sin.' " Jung's comments on the beginning of the vision are as follows:

> It is significant that what comes to him is no erotic phantasy. . . . His mistress appears before him . . . in "divine" form, seeming to him like a goddess in the heavens. This fact indicates that the repressed erotic impression in the unconscious had activated the latent primordial image of the goddess, which is in fact the archetypal soul-image.[44]

Jung had, elsewhere, defined "soul-image" as "the inner attitude of the unconscious . . . represented by definite persons whose particular qualities correspond with those of the soul." And, on the basis of the principle of complementarity, "for a man, a woman is best fitted to be the bearer of his soul-image." It is, in effect, an image of one's own "inner psychic processes."[45]

Jung's analysis of what happened to Hermas, then, is that "the repressed erotic impression in the unconscious" had "become united in the collective unconscious with those archaic residues which from primordial time have held the imprints of woman's nature; woman as mother, and woman as desirable maid. Such impressions have immense power, since they release forces, both in the child and the man, which, in their irresistible and absolutely compelling nature, merit the attribute divine."

In the next stage of the vision, Rhoda is transformed into an old woman "in shining garments"; and it is revealed to Hermas that this old woman is the *Church*, "whereby," Jung writes, "the concrete and personal is dissolved into an abstraction and the ideal gains an actuality and a reality which it had never before possessed." The old woman bids Hermas to a trysting-place where he is put to trial for his sin, and his means of expiation is revealed to him as a mission to be fulfilled. Jung's analysis proceeds on the following principles:

> . . . if, against the wholly overwhelming power of passion, which casts a man unconditionally in the path of another, the psyche succeeds in erecting a counterposition, whereby at the summit of passion it severs the idol from the utterly desired object and forces the man to his knees before the divine image, it has thereby delivered him from the curse of the object's spell. He is restored again to himself; he is even forced upon himself, thus coming once more into his own way between gods and men, and subject to his own laws.

Such recognition of a soul-image, therefore, is not due to moral repression, but rather to "a self-regulation of the psychic organism which seeks by this orientation to protect itself from loss of equilibrium." Consequently:

> This mechanism is clearly effective in the case of Hermas. The transformation of Rhoda into the

divine mistress deprives the actual object of her pro-
vocative and destructive power, and brings Hermas
under the law of his own soul and its collective determinants. . . . Through the conversion of a possible
social trespass and a probable passional self-injury
to the service of the soul, Hermas is guided to the
accomplishment of a social task of a spiritual nature,
which for that time was, assuredly, of no small importance.

By the transformation of Rhoda into a symbol of the
Church, the erotic element recedes into the background,
while Hermas' investments in the values of the Church
are enhanced. Following upon the trials, Hermas is confronted by the vision of ten thousand youths and men
building a tower — to which it is his mission to contribute. In effect, the passional mistress is transformed into
the Church-as-mistress more worthy of his soul-image,
and the Church becomes symbolized by the *tower*. This
edifice, built of stones perfectly fitted together without
joints, possesses the security and steadfastness which, in
his conscious life, Hermas had been laboring to establish
for the young and divisively torn group of Christian
believers.

It is this tower in Hermas' book of visions that Jung
is concerned with interpreting symbolically, as an expression of an archetype of the collective unconscious.
It possesses the associations of the tower-attributes of the
Virgin ascribed to her in the Litany of Loretto; of the
security of the tower (God) referred to in the *Psalms*,
lvi, 4; of the Tower of Babel insofar as Hermas "suffered

much from the depressing spectacle of the ceaseless schisms and heretical strifes of the Early Church." But what are the links which connect the old woman as symbol of the Church with the tower symbol?

Like the lines of the Lorettian Litany, this image of "tower" has its source in *The Song of Songs*. While the poem was originally a secular love-song, "mystical interpretation . . . always loved to conceive the bride as Israel and the bridegroom as Jehovah, and indeed, from a right instinct; since the aim of this conception is a translation of the erotic emotion into a national relationship with God." The erotic nature of the tower similes in *The Song of Songs* was accepted by the Church Fathers. St. Ambrose and St. Augustine, subsequently, wrote of the images of the towers in *The Song of Songs* in which womb, vessel, and tower are clearly associated.

But the vessel-symbolism has extra-Biblical origins, as well. "The fact that the vessel-symbol is certainly very ancient . . . [involves comparisons] moulded upon pagan models . . . Mithraic prototype . . . well-known and widely spread Gnostic vessel-symbolism of that time. . . . The fertilizing activity of the pitcher . . . expressed in antique phraseology as the 'impregnation of Isis by the seed of Osiris.'" In other words, expressions are found both in primitive peoples today and in manifestations as old as early Egyptian images of the vessel connected with the uterus, and the concept of the growth of life in that which has been fertilized. In the history of Christianity, acceptance of the vessel symbol by the Fathers of the Church looks backward to images of paganism ("since the Virgin worship is itself a vestige of paganism, by which the

Christian Church secured the entail of the Magna Mater, Isis, and others") as well as forward to the legend of the Grail which "contains considerable psychological enlightenment in its relation to the service of woman." Since the vessel image is non-Christian in origin:

> The survival, or unconscious revivification of the vessel-symbol indicates a strengthening of the feminine principle in the masculine psychology of that time. This symbolization by means of a mysterious image must be interpreted as a spiritualizing of the erotic motive evoked by the service of woman. But spiritual transformation always means the holding back of a sum of libido, which would otherwise be immediately squandered in sexuality. Experience shows that, when a sum of libido is thus retained, one part of it flows into the spiritualized expression, while the remainder sinks into the unconscious, where it effects a certain activation of corresponding images of which this vessel symbolism is the expression.

This, then, is the line of analysis used by Jung in reference to *The Shepherd*. Hermas' concern moves from the actual woman, Rhoda, in whom his soul-image is lodged, to the old woman — as the Church — to the tower, as the symbol of the Church given a unified, powerful, and secure existence.

> The detachment of the libido from the real object, its translation into the symbol and conversion into a symbolic function, is thus completed. Hence-

86

forth the idea of a universal and undivided Church, expressed in the symbol of a jointless and immovable tower, becomes an unshakable reality in the mind of Hermas.

The symbolic function is here seen to operate as a genuine transcendence or synthesis of the tension between opposites which issues into the capacity to do further "effective work" on the basis of a relative subjective freedom of action. The symbol-forming process has been connected with the source of all affective power: the archetypes of the collective unconscious. Jung remarks in a summary passage:

> This is not to be marvelled at, since these images are deposits, representing the accumulated experience of thousands of years of struggle for adaptation and existence. Every great experience of life, every profound conflict, evokes the treasured wealth of these images and brings them to inner perception; as such, they become accessible to unconsciousness only in the presence of that degree of self-awareness and power of understanding which enables a man also to think what he experiences instead of just living it blindly. In the latter case he actually lives the myth and the symbol without knowing it.[46]

We are now in a position to consider directly the application of Jung's conceptions to the theory of art.

PART

II

Outline *of a*
Jungian Aesthetics

Jung considers that Freud's contribution to aesthetics is only another instance of the genetic fallacy. "It is his art that explains the artist," Jung writes, "and not the insufficiencies and conflicts of his personal life"[1] which explain his art.

It is, therefore, necessary to represent Jung's negative judgment on Freud's conceptions concerning art before proceeding to Jung's own position.

> Freud thought that he had found a key in his procedure of deriving the work of art from the personal experiences of the artist. It is true that certain possibilities lay in this direction, for it was conceivable that a work of art, no less than a neurosis might be traced back to those knots in psychic life we call the

91

complexes. . . . Freud takes the neurosis as a substitute for a direct means of gratification. He therefore
regards it as something inappropriate — a mistake, a
dodge, an excuse, a voluntary blindness. . . . And a
work of art is brought into questionable proximity
with the neurosis when it is taken as something which
can be analysed in terms of the poet's repressions.[2]

That the poet's "disposition" permeates his works of
art, goes without saying. But Jung's idea is that this tru-
ism adds nothing new or psychologically significant to
the interpretation of art. That the materials and the techniques chosen by the artist have been influenced by personal factors, is for him tautologous with saying that the
artist *qua* human being has had particular experiences and
qua artist has had training in the techniques and intentions of some artistic discipline and school of thought.

No objection can be raised if it is admitted that
this approach [of Freudian psychology] amounts to
nothing more than the elucidation of those personal
determinants without which a work of art is unthink-
able. But should the claim be made that such an
analysis *accounts for the work of art itself*, then a
categorical denial is called for.[3]

Such "personal determinants" are, for Jung, extremely
questionable in value for aesthetics, as the idiosyncratic
(what contemporary critics call the "private reference")
is not essential to the work of art. "In fact, the more
we have to cope with these peculiarities, the less is it a
question of art. What is essential in a work of art is that

it should rise far above the realm of personal life and speak from the spirit and heart of the poet as man to the spirit and heart of mankind. The personal aspect is a limitation — and even a sin — in the realm of art."

The essence of Jung's criticism is that Freud's method is not valueless in its application to certain works of art, but that it has been extended beyond the scope of its usefulness and that its overextension is self-defeating. The scope of its usefulness is, precisely, the realm of bad art, for that is where idiosyncratic peculiarities predominate over what is essential to a good work of art. Jung maintains that psychology can tell us nothing about the special character of artistic as compared with scientific, political, or religious *creativity*, *if* it concentrates on the similarities among the individual psychologies of such "creators." In other words, his criticism amounts to an attack on the Freudian idea that these differentiated activities are all "in the last analysis" explained by being traced back to the same structures of psychic economy.

> For if we go back far enough in the state of mental development for the essential differences of the individual provinces of the mind to have become altogether invisible, we have not thereby reached a deeper principle of their unity, but merely an earlier evolutionary state of undifferentiation in which neither province has as yet any existence at all.[4]

This intention — the pursuit of "the last analysis" — characterizes the Freudian attempt in its effort to make of psychology a science in the sense of 19th century physical science, where "the scientific attitude will naturally and constantly tend to overlook the nature of a differentiation in favour of its causal derivation, and will strive to subordinate the former to an idea that is certainly more general, but at the same time more elementary."

However, Jung argues, application of this method and Freud's principles to the subject matter of art is *inappropriate* because, by the reduction to so-called elementary conditions, "nothing is gained by this procedure for the understanding of his art, since we can perform the same reduction in every other possible case, and not the least in cases of pathological disorder. Neurosis and psychosis are also reducible to infantile relations with the parents, as are good and bad habits, convictions, qualities, passions, especial interests, and so forth. But we are surely not entitled to assume that all these very different things must, therefore, have one and the same explanation; for were that so, we should be driven to conclude that they were actually one and the same thing. Thus, if a work of art and a neurosis are explained in precisely similar terms, either the work of art must be a neurosis, or the neurosis a work of art." The criticism is stated so that if Jung had been writing in Aristotelian language he could say: Freud's position makes it appear that the assumed material and efficient causes are exhaustive for explanation; formal and final causes would be meaningless if not simply unimportant.

To say that the origins of certain works of art have the same psychological pre-conditions as the origins of certain neuroses means, for Jung, only that:

> . . . certain psychic preconditions are universally

94

present, and furthermore, because of the relative similarity of human conditions of life these are constantly the same, whether in the case of a nervous
intellectual, a poet, or a normal human being. . . .
That one poet is influenced more by the relation to
the father, another by the tie to the mother, while the
third reveals unmistakable traces of repressed sexuality in his works — all this can be said equally well
not only of every neurotic, but also of every normal
human being. Hence nothing specific is thereby
gained for the judgment of a work of art.

Jung's conclusion, therefore, is that while Freud's medical psychology may enable the researcher to "broaden
and deepen" his knowledge of universal preconditions,
and to make a more "penetrating and exhaustive demon-
stration" of their influences on the way in which the
particular personal life of the artist —"reaching back even
as far as earliest childhood"— is interwoven in his artistic
creations, this is a development only in *degree* of the kind
of psychologico-literary analysis which existed prior to
Freud. Jung may be thinking here particularly of Charles
Augustin Saint-Beuve (1804-1869) who developed the
approach to literary criticism which requires that the
work of art must not be examined independent of careful
research into the biography of the writer. Among distinguished critics of today Edmund Wilson is the best
known practitioner of this technique.

The Freudian development in degree of this psychologico-literary tradition brings with it, Jung remarks, a
certain loss of good taste or discretion. "This lack of deli-

95

cacy in dealing with the all-too-human element, . . . [has the effect that] our interest is unwittingly diverted from the work of art and gets lost in the mazy, labyrinthine confusion of psychic preconditions, the poet becomes a clinical case, even serving on occasion as a curious example of *psychopathia sexualis*. But therewith the psychoanalysis of the art-work has also turned aside from its objective, and the discussion has strayed into a province that is as broad as mankind, and not in the smallest degree specific for the artist; it therefore possesses even less relevance to his art."

Freud's method consists in this: it is

> . . . a medico-psychological technique for the investigation of morbid psychic phenomena. This technique is exclusively occupied with the ways and means for circumventing or peering through the conscious foreground in order to reach the so-called unconscious, or psychic background. It is based upon the assumption that the neurotic patient is repressing certain psychic contents from consciousness because of their incompatibility or inconsistency with conscious values. This incompatibility is regarded as a moral one; accordingly, the repressed contents must bear a corresponding negative character, namely, infantile-sexual, obscene, or even criminal. It is these qualities that render them so distasteful to consciousness. Since no man is perfect, it is clear that everyone must possess such a background whether the fact be admitted or not. Hence it can be disclosed in all cases if only we apply the technique of interpreta-

tion elaborated by Freud.[5]

This method of Freud's is a therapeutic one developed for the cure of "morbid and unsuitable" psychological structures. Since such a neurosis has "taken the place of normal accomplishment . . . [it] must be broken down before the way can be cleared for a sound adaptation. In this case the process of leading-back to a general human basis is entirely appropriate." But what happens when this method is applied to works of art?

> From beneath the shimmering robe of art it extracts the naked commonness of the elementary *homo sapiens*, to which species the poet also belongs. The golden semblance of sublime creation we were about to discuss is blotted out; for its essence is lost when we treat it with the corrosive method which has to be used for the deceptive phantasms of hysteria.

If a consequence of applying this method to the study of art results in such a Freudian principle as "every artist is a narcissist"— has any contribution been made to aesthetics? Jung asks whether it is permissible to use such a concept as "narcissist," for example, which was coined specifically to describe a neurotic psycho-pathology as descriptive for psychological activity so much more broadly conceived. And, even if it were justifiable, then it could equally well be applied to "every man who pursues his own line to the limit of his powers"; in which case, every scientist, every religious leader, every social reformer, *et al.*, is equally "a narcissist." But, again, nothing specific has been gained for the understanding of art.

97

Despite the fact that Freud may have believed that his method would reveal the answer to the question of why works of art have the affective power which they have, in fact, what this method produces is a devaluation of the nature of art itself. What it yields is nothing more than a summary of arguments to prove that artists are also human beings, victims or heroes depending on how they have responded to the universal conditions of "the family romance."

What is crucial for understanding Jung's criticism of Freud can now be stated in the light of the differences between their theories of symbolism. For Freud: the unconscious background in each individual psyche "does not remain inactive, but betrays itself in certain characteristic effects upon the conscious content. For example, it creates phantasy-products of a peculiar character . . . disturbances of the conscious process . . . [and] dreams."

> The essential factor of Freud's reductive method consists in the fact that it collects all the circumstantial evidence of the unconscious backgrounds, and, through the analysis and interpretation of the material, reconstructs the elementary unconscious, instinctive processes. Those conscious contents which give us a clue, as it were, to the unconscious backgrounds are by Freud incorrectly termed symbols.

We are already familiar with Jung's criticism of this conception. For Jung, those contents that are clues must be considered signs or symptoms of the background processes which may be conceived as "better known." Only expressions of "intuitive perceptions" of a subject matter which "can as yet, neither be apprehended better, nor expressed differently," are, for Jung, symbols properly so-called.

Jung gives the examples of Jesus's "Kingdom of Heaven" and of Plato's metaphor of "The Cave" as instances of genuine symbols which attempt "to express a thing, for which there exists as yet no adequate verbal concept." If one were to take the symbolic expression by which Plato presents his theory of cognition and apply to it Freud's method for interpretation,

> . . . we should naturally come to the uterus, and we should have proved that even the mind of Plato was deeply stuck in the primeval levels of 'infantile sexuality.' But in doing so we should also remain in total ignorance of what Plato actually created from the primitive antecedents of his philosophical intuition; we should, in fact, carelessly have overlooked his most essential product, merely to discover that he had 'infantile' phantasies like every other mortal. Such a conclusion could possess value only for the man who regards Plato as a *superhuman* being, and who is therefore able to find a certain satisfaction in the fact that even Plato was also a man. . . . But *this* would have *nothing whatever* to do with the *meaning* of the Platonic parable.[6]

In other words, the achievement possible to the application of Freudian principles and method to works of art is to disclose the material and efficient causes of the product in the same terms by which a neurosis is explained.

99

What is lost by the limitations of such medical-psychol-ogy, Jung wishes to compensate for by concentrating on the prospective meaning of the work of art — not in re-duction to such material and efficient causation, nor by invasion of the realm of formal causes (i.e., he is not an art critic, nor does he mean to discount the independent importance of formal art criticism) — but by what should properly be called final causation. For example, if the subject under consideration were the metaphor of "The Cave" of Plato, again, the analysis of its formal cause would be the province of philosophy, the job of phil-osophic critics; but what Jung would be concerned about there would be to consider what light analytic psychol-ogy can shed on its psychological meaning, independent of both the causally-reductive analysis of material and efficient cause in respect to the psyche of the philosopher-artist, and the formal analysis of the intellectual meaning made by philosopher-critics. The psychological meaning as *aim* or *purpose* or *goal* of the psychic achievement is independent of its relations to the personal factors in the life of its creator; whereas, it is very much more closely related to its aesthetic (or intellectual) formal causes. But analysis of the formal causes in the evaluation of works of art rests in the hands of art critics. Jung states, in this respect: ". . . that which constitutes the essential nature of art must always lie outside [psychology's] province."

What is proper to psychology is not to mistake the work of art for a human being and "explain it away" in a manner comparable to treating the neurosis of a hu-man being. Rather, Jung's contention is that, the proper concern of psychology is not with the personal conditions of creation but with the psychic significance of the work of art. Only after considering the question of what psychology can contribute to the understanding of art from that point of view can one, subsequently, turn attention to the role which creativity plays in the life of the artist and the function it serves in the psychic life of the audience.

The doubt may be raised as to whether art does have meaning, ". . . whether in fact art does 'signify'."

> Perhaps art itself does not intend to "signify," contains no sort of "meaning," at least not in the sense in which we are now speaking of "meaning." Perhaps it is like nature, which simply is, without any intention to "signify." . . . But when we are speaking of the relation of psychology to the work of art we are standing outside of the realm of art, and here it is impossible for us not to speculate. . . . we must find meaning in things, otherwise we should be quite unable to think about them. We must resolve life and happenings, all that fulfills itself in itself, into images, meanings, concepts. . . . And in so doing, what was before pure phenomenon, becomes something that in association with other phenomena has meaning; it plays a definite role, serves certain ends, brings about effects fraught with meaning. And when we can see all this we get the feeling of having understood and explained something. Thus is the need of science recognized.[7]

In other words, Jung conceives the primary concern of an analytic psychological interpretation of art to be with the nature of the psychic significance of works of art; and this, in respect to making the connections between a theory of human psychology and the phenomena of works of art, is achieved, not by beginning with the process of the artist's act of creation, but by an inquiry into the different "roles," "ends," and "effects" of works of art. *It is analysis in terms of final cause.*

This sense in which Jung is now speaking of "meaning," and which I shall call "psychic significance," is based on Jung's theory of symbolism. The end, aim or goal of symbols as distinguished from signs has been characterized teleologically, mediating between consciousness and the Collective Unconscious; symbols being such psychic phenomena as contain – potentially – prospective purport for the on-going development of the individual's integration. For his inquiry into what ideas psychology can contribute to the study of art, *Jung makes his key hypothesis the idea that a certain kind of art functions for a society in a way analogous with the function of "private" symbols in individual psychology.*

The first product of such inquiry, Jung calls "psychological phenomenology." What he does is to elaborate a typology, a division of two classes into which he argues it will be found that all works of (poetic) art may be distinguished. It must be remembered that Jung's criticism of Freud's position amounts to this: "The assumptions it rests upon are quite arbitrary. In no sense, for example, are neuroses exclusively based upon sexual repression, and the same holds good for psychoses. There is no foundation for saying that dreams merely contain repressed wishes the incompatibility of which requires them to be disguised by a hypothetical dream-censor. The Freudian technique, insofar as it remains under the influence of its own one-sided and, therefore, erroneous hypotheses, is patently arbitrary."

In criticism of what Jung considers Freud's limitations, we have already introduced the two most significant of Jung's innovations in connection with his (a) distinction to be made between signs and symbols, and (b) his division within the field of the unconscious between the contents of personal and collective unconsciousness. It may now be seen how these principles, when applied to the examination of art, will yield a strikingly different outline for aesthetics. The two essays in which Jung attempted to draw this outline are specifically concerned with literary art, although they can be taken as paradigms for the way in which the extensive references to the graphic and plastic works of art, found throughout Jung's numerous volumes, likewise could be systematically treated. I am referring, of course, to the essay entitled *On the Relation of Analytical Psychology to Poetic Art*, originally read before the Gesellschaft für deutsche Sprache und Literatur, in Zürich, May, 1922,[8] and the essay called *Psychology and Literature*, originally published in *Die Philosophie der Literaturwissenschaft*, edited by Ermatinger, Junker and Dünnhaut, Berlin, 1929.[9]

SECTION 2: *The Work of Art*

What Jung calls his "psychological phenomenological" treatment of art is the construction of a typology helping to serve an inquiry into the psychic significance of art.

He finds that, with varying degrees of certainty, all works of literary art can be judged to belong to one of two classes. The first class is of such a nature that, as far as its meaning is concerned: "... there is nothing that the psychologist can add to it that the poet has not already said in better words."[10] The second class contains works of which "the prodigious richness of the imaginative material has so overtaxed the poet's formative powers that nothing is self-explanatory and every verse adds to the reader's need of an interpretation." Jung writes that "I will call the one mode of artistic creation *psychological,* and the other *visionary.*"

What gives Jung warrant then to speak of a "psychological phenomenology" is the fact that he elucidates this classification in respect to (a) subject matter and (b) method of artistic creation.

I. THE PSYCHOLOGICAL MODE

(a) *Subject Matter.* Here the materials that works of art are "about" are "drawn from the realm of human consciousness—for instance, [from] the lessons of life, with emotional shocks, the experience of passion and the crises of human destiny in general—all of which go to make up the conscious life of man, and his feeling life in particular." "Countless literary works belong to this class: the many novels dealing with love, the environment, the family, crime and society, as well as didactic poetry, the larger number of lyrics, and the drama both tragic and comic. Whatever its particular form may be, the psychological work of art always takes its materials from the vast realm of conscious human experience—from the vivid foreground of life, we might say."

Jung states: "I have called this mode of artistic creation psychological because in its activity it nowhere transcends the bounds of psychological intelligibility. Everything that it embraces—the experience as well as its artistic expression—belongs to the realm of the understandable. Even the basic experiences themselves, though non-rational, have nothing strange about them; on the contrary, they are that which has been known from the beginning of time—passion and its fated outcome, man's subjection to the turns of destiny, eternal nature with its beauty and its horror."

(b) *Method.* "In this case the author submits his material to a defiinite treatment that is both directed and purposeful; he adds to it and subtracts from it, emphasizing one effect, modifying another, laying on this color here, that there, with the most careful weighing of their possible effects, and with the constant observance of the laws of beautiful form and style. To this labour the author brings his keenest judgment, and selects his expression with the most complete freedom. In his view his material is only material, and entirely subject to his artistic purpose; he wills to present this and nothing else."[11]

Furthermore, "this material is psychically assimilated by the poet, raised from the commonplace to the level of poetic experience, and given an expression which forces the reader to greater clarity and depth of human insight by bringing fully into his consciousness what he ordinarily evades and overlooks or senses only with a feeling of dull discomfort. The poet's work is an interpretation and illumination of the contents of consciousness, of the ineluctable experiences of human life with its eternally recurrent sorrow and joy."[12] By contrast now, in the language of extremes, the visionary mode "reverses all the conditions" of the psychological mode.

II. THE VISIONARY MODE

(a) *Subject Matter.* "The experience that furnishes the material for artistic expression is no longer familiar. It is a strange something that derives its existence from the hinterland of man's mind—that suggests the abyss of time separating us from pre-human ages, or evokes a super-human world of contrasting light and darkness. It is a primordial experience which surpasses man's understanding, and to which he is therefore in danger of succumbing. The value and the force of the experience are given by its enormity. It arises from the timeless depths; it is foreign and cold, many-sided, demonic and grotesque. . . . The disturbing vision of monstrous and meaningless happenings that in every way exceed the grasp of human feeling and comprehension makes quite other demands upon the powers of the artist than do the experiences of the foreground of life. These never rend the curtain that veils the cosmos; they never transcend the bounds of the humanly possible, and for this reason are readily shaped to the demands of art, no matter how great a shock to the individual they may be. But the primordial experiences rend from top to bottom the curtain upon which is painted the picture of an ordered world, and allow a glimpse into the unfathomed abyss of what has not yet become. Is it a vision of another world, or of the obscuration of the spirit, or of the beginning of things before the age of man, or of the unborn generations of the future? We cannot say that it is any or none of these."

(b) *Method*. "These works positively impose themselves upon the author; his hand is, as it were, seized, and his pen writes things that his mind perceives with amazement. The work brings with it its own form; what he would add to it is declined, what he does not wish to admit is forced upon him. While his consciousness stands disconcerted and empty before the phenomenon, he is overwhelmed with a flood of thoughts and images which it was never his aim to beget and which his will would never have fashioned. Yet in spite of himself he is forced to recognize that in all this his self is speaking, that his innermost nature is revealing itself, uttering things that he would never have entrusted to his tongue. He can only obey and follow the apparently foreign impulse, feeling that his work is greater than himself, and therefore has a power over him that he is quite unable to command."[13]

Jung insists that in describing these contrasting materials and methods he is not concerned with the poet as a person (whose particular psychogenic history is necessarily involved) but rather only with "the creative process that moves him." In criticism of Freud, Jung had argued:

> A purely causalistic psychology is only able to reduce every human individual to a member of the species *homo sapiens*, since its entire range is limited to what is either transmitted or derived. But the artwork is not merely transmitted or derived—it is a creative reorganization of those very determinants to which a causalistic psychology must always re-

107

duce it. . . . The art-work must be regarded as a
creative formation, freely making use of every pre-
condition. Its meaning and its own individual par-
ticularity rests in itself, and not in its preconditions.

When Jung distinguishes between two modes of artistic creation, he therefore contrasts the ways in which
artists themselves speak of their relation to the creative
process. In the case of the Psychological Mode, "the poet
is simply identical with the creative process, whether he
has willingly surrendered himself as the head of the creative movement, or whether this has so entirely seized
upon him as a tool or instrument that all consciousness of
the fact has escaped him. He is the creative process itself,
standing completely in it and undifferentiated from it
with all his aims and all his powers."

In the caes of the Visionary Mode, the poet ". . . is not
identical with the process of creative formation; he is himself conscious of the fact that he stands as it were under-
neath his work, or at all events beside it, as though he
were another person who had fallen within the magic
circle of an alien will." While this may sound very much
like the contrast characterized by Schiller as "Senti-
mental" and "Naive," as Jung had re-presented it in
Psychological Types, he makes the following extensions
here on the basis of his general theory. "Psychologically
we term [the Sentimental] introverted, [the Naive] extroverted." Referring to the kind of creative process
typical of the Psychological Mode, Jung then writes,
"The introverted attitude is characterized by an uphold-
ing of the subject with his conscious ends and aims against

the claims and pretensions of the object; the extroverted attitude on the contrary, is distinguished by a subordination of the subject to the claims of the object." The latter, would then be descriptive of the creative process of the Visionary Mode. In the Psychological Mode "the material is mastered by the aim of the poet." In the Visionary, "the material distinguishes itself by its refractory obstinacy."[14]

As with any psychological typology, the contrast established here between the two literary modes is not to be mistaken for a division between two water-tight compartments. There is "leakage" or "seepage" from one to the other; there is a twilight zone between the two — to mix a metaphor. Consequently, qualifications must be made with respect to the interpretations which artists themselves put on the nature of their creative processes.

The problem lies with the degree of psychological activity or passivity. An author may conceive himself to be the active agent (in the Psychological Mode) "... he is perhaps fully convinced of his own freedom, and will not be disposed to allow that his creation is not also his will, from which, in conjunction with his knowledge, he believes it to be exclusively derived." On the other hand, an author may think of himself as a passive agent (in the Visionary Mode) having no "... direct appreciation of his own will in the apparently foreign inspiration, and notwithstanding the fact that it is manifestly the voice of his own self."

Here we are faced with a question that we are quite unable to answer from what the poet himself

109

tells us about the manner of his creating. It is really a scientific problem that psychology alone can solve.

In the former case, it may well be that "the poet, while apparently creating consciously and spontaneously out of himself and producing only what he intends, is nevertheless, in spite of his consciousness, so caught up by the creative impulse that he is as little aware of an 'alien' will," as the poet in the latter case is aware of the influence which his conscious past has contributed. Jung cites as "direct proof" of the misconception in the case of the poet in the Psychological Mode instances "where the poet, in what he believes he is saying, actually and patently says more than he himself is aware of.... Indirect proof would be found in cases, where behind the apparent spontaneity of the production there stands a higher 'must,' that reveals the imperative nature of its demand if the creative activity is renounced voluntarily, or in those difficult psychic complications which immediately ensue in the event of an arbitrary interruption of the artistic production." That is, the first kind of evidence is taken from a consideration of the subject matter, the second from a study of the process of creation.

Similarly with the author's conception of his passivity in the Visionary Mode. What the poet has done is to minimize the role of his consciousness—will, intention, and history of acquired technique—in the light of what is taken to be the overwhelming experience of the art-work, describing *it* ".... as a being that uses man and his personal dispositions merely as a cultural medium or soil, disposing his powers according to its own laws, while shaping itself to the fulfilment of its own creative purpose."

In effect, therefore, the difference between the two modes of creation is a difference only of degree, which might be summarized in the following way. Depending on whether the author experiences more intensely his awareness of exerting conscious shaping control over his subject matter or his awareness of being controlled by the subject matter—he will present his idea of the process by which he created the art-work as active or passive. But Jung's point is that in both modes there is evidence of passivity. It is only the case that one working in the Visionary Mode is *more* conscious of an 'alien' will or an intention beyond his comprehension. Therefore, while one can employ such "evidence" as this, from the auto-biographical statements of authors, in constructing a general psychological phenomenology, and while such distinctions are helpful as hints, they are not sufficient to what psychology must investigate in order to contribute to aesthetics. It is Jung's purpose then to show in what sense the artist's manner of creating is "a scientific problem that psychology alone can solve."

Since he has been maintaining that it is not the poet as a person with whom he is concerned but with the creative process that moves him, the question for Jung is: "... what contribution can analytical psychology make to the root-problem of artistic 'creation,' that is, the mystery of the creative energy?"

SECTION 3: *Creative Energy*

What explains that aspect of the artist's experience which

he characterizes as passive? "The unborn work in the soul of the artist is a force of nature that effects its purpose, either with tyrannical might, or with the subtle cunning which nature brings to the achievement of her end, quite regardless of the personal weal or woe of the man who is the vehicle of the creative force. The creative energy lives and waxes in the man as a tree in the earth from which it takes nourishment. It might be well, therefore, to regard the creative process as a living thing, implanted, as it were, in the souls of men."

Jung uses a second figure of speech to compare the growth of a work of art to the development of a child in its mother's womb. "But there is a certain lameness about all comparisons; in place of metaphors therefore, let us make use of the more precise terminology of science."

> In terms of analytical psychology this is *an autonomous complex*. It is in fact a detached portion of the psyche that leads an independent psychic life withdrawn from the hierarchy of consciousness, and in proportion to its energic value or force, may appear as a mere disturbance of the voluntarily directed process of consciousness, or as a superordinated authority which may take the ego bodily into its service.[15]

In respect to the two modes of creating, the latter case would describe the process for the poet "who is identified with the creative process and who at once acquiesces whenever the unconscious 'must' threaterns," i.e., in the Psychological Mode. "But the other poet, to whom the creative element appears almost as a foreign power, is unable for one reason or another to acquiesce, and is, accordingly, caught by the 'must' unawares," i.e., in the Visionary Mode. To anticipate certain of Jung's remarks on the artist, which will be developed later, it may be seen in this light why the artist who creates in the Psychological Mode will appear as a more integrated person, and why the artist who creates in the Visionary Mode appears "unbalanced."

> You will remember that I described the work existing *in statu nascendi as an* autonomous complex. This concept is used to distinguish all those psychic formations which at first are developed quite unconsciously, and only from the moment when they attain threshold-value are able to break through into consciousness.[16]

The result is that when such a break-through into consciousness is made, the contents of the complex are not experienced as assimilated material but, rather, associated with consciousness of a *perception.* This, in effect, means that such contents are not available for subjection to conscious control, being neither inhibitable nor available for "reappearance" at will. The autonomy of such a complex is revealed precisely in the fact that it appears or vanishes "when and in such guise as accords with its own intrinsic tendency."

Jung's thesis is that: "the creative complex shares this peculiarity with every other autonomous complex." This is not to say that Freud's contention is acceptable for a general aesthetics—that the function of artistic creation serves the same psychic purpose as a neurosis—despite the fact that neuroses, also, "are especially distinguished by the appearance of autonomous complexes." Jung points out that the relationship between the two is an analogy, not that of identity. But the fact that "the divine frenzy of the artist" is analogous to the activation of a neurosis:

> proves nothing either for or against the morbid hypothesis, since normal men have also to submit either temporarily or permanently to the tyranny of autonomous complexes. The fact is simply one of the normal peculiarities of the psyche.... For instance every typical attitude that is to a certain extent differentiated shows a tendency to become an autonomous complex, and in the majority of cases actually becomes one. Every instinct too has more or less the character of an autonomous complex. In itself, therefore, there is nothing morbid in an autonomous complex, only its stored-up energy and its disturbing appearance on the scene may often involve suffering or illness.

An autonomous complex develops when psychic energy has been withdrawn from conscious control. Whatever the efficient cause which occasions such a withdrawal, "a hitherto unconscious region of the psyche is thrown into activity, and this activation undergoes a certain development and extension through the inclusion of related associations." Either consciousness then identifies itself with the complex or "there results what Janet has termed an *'abaissement du niveau mental'*." In the latter case:

The intensity of conscious interests and activities gradually fades, whereupon, either an apathetic inactivity—a condition very common with artists— or a regressive development of the conscious functions takes place, namely, a descent to their infantile or archaic pre-stages; hence something akin to a degeneration. The *'parties inférieures des functions'* force themselves to the front, the instinctive rather than the ethical, the naively infantile instead of the deliberated and mature, the unadapted in place of the adapted. This also is shown in the lives of many artists.

But, since autonomous complexes are something to which "normal men have also to submit," the question must be asked: "in what does the autonomous *creative* complex consist?" The only means which Jung finds for answering the question requires that he work backward from the finished art-work to the creative process. It is the production of works of art which distinguish the artist, after all, not the presence of autonomous complexes which make either normal men or neurotics into artists. Jung's handling of the answer is, then, determined by the kind of art on which he focuses his investigation. "We can know next to nothing," he writes, of the autonomous *creative* complex, "so long as the completed work offers us no insight into its foundations." Apparently, there are such works as do offer an insight, and those which do not. One may see, now, how the phenomenological distinction between the Psychological and the Visionary modes will be put to use.

The work gives us a finished picture in the widest sense. This picture is accessible to analysis just insofar as we are able to appreciate it as a *symbol*. But if we are unable to discover any symbolic value in it, we have thereby ascertained that, for us at least, it means no more than what it obviously says . . . it is no more than it seems.

At face value, now, it would appear that Jung is identifying art-works in the Psychological Mode with the class of completed works that "means no more than it obviously says"; and art-works in the Visionary Mode with the class in which completed works can be appreciated as having "symbolic value." However, he offers two qualifications. The first is the confession that "it is conceivable that our own bias forbids a wider appreciation" (of the former class). The second is, it may be the case that the symbolic qualities "remain hidden." This could occur when a work of art apparently in the Psychological Mode also possesses symbolic qualities "passing into the indefinable and thus transcending contemporary consciousness" such that neither the author nor the readers take it to mean more than it says. But this is relative to the author's consciousness and to the spirit of the time. In this connection, whether one speaks of the author or of his audience:

> [one] moves within the limits of contemporary consciousness, with small hope of availing himself of some Archimedian point outside the orbit of his world by which he could raise, as it were, his contemporary consciousness off its hinges. For nothing

short of this would enable him to recognize the symbol in a work of this kind; the symbol being the possibility and intimation of a meaning higher and wider than our present powers of comprehension can seize.

Jung points out that he makes this qualification so that "the possible significance of a work of art might not be fettered or restricted by my typification, even though apparently it intends neither to be nor to say anything except what it obviously is and says." And he supports this qualification with the evidence from the history of literary criticism in which "a poet long dead is suddenly rediscovered."

This may occur when our conscious development has reached a higher level, from which standpoint the ancient poet can tell us something new. It was always present in his work, but it remained a hidden symbol that only a renewal of the spirit of the time permits us to read and to understand. It demanded other and fresher eyes, just because the old ones could see in it only the things they were accustomed to see. Experiences like these should prompt us to be circumspect. . . .

In effect, the distinction between the Psychological and the Visionary Modes not being absolute, it is the function of the literary or of the psychological critic to discern the symbolic value of any given work of art. One may recall, in this connection, Jung's remarks presented earlier on the interpretive disposition he calls "the symbolic attitude."

These qualifications notwithstanding, for his immediate practical purposes, Jung writes as though it is only art-works in the Visionary Mode—i.e., which have symbolic value—that can be a source of the insight he is seeking into the autonomous creative complex. In such works of art, he asserts that we recognize ". . . something of a supra-personal character that transcends the range of conscious understanding in the same degree as the author's consciousness is withheld from the development of his work. We should expect a certain strangeness of form and shape, thoughts that can only be apprehended by intuition, a language pregnant with meanings, expressions that would have the value of genuine symbols, because they are the best possible expressions of something as yet unknown—bridges thrown out toward an invisible shore." "Here we may lay our hand upon the symbol, although a satisfying solution of the riddle still escapes us."

The question of the nature of the autonomous *creative* complex, then, translated into Jung's psychological language, becomes: ". . . to what primordial image of the collective unconscious can we trace the image we see developed in the [Symbolic] work of art?"

> This question demands elucidation in more than one respect. As already observed, the case I have assumed is that of a symbolical art-work; a work, therefore, of which the source is not to be found in the personal unconscious of the author, but in the sphere of unconscious mythology, the primordial contents of which are the common heritage of mankind. Accordingly, I have termed this sphere the

118

collective unconscious, thus distinguishing it from a personal unconscious which I regard as the totality of those psychic processes and contents that are not only accessible to consciousness, but often would be conscious were they not subject to repression. . . .

SECTION 4: *The Psychic Significance of Art-Works and the Creative Process*

Jung argues for his distinction between two modes of art on the basis of differences between the "subject matters" found in actual art-works. In the Psychological Mode, the material presented "nowhere transcends the bounds of psychological intelligibility."[17] In the Visionary Mode, the material presented offers an "experience which surpasses man's understanding."[18] The result of this is that the two hold entirely different psychic significances for the audience. ". . . The symbolical work is more stimulating, drives, as it were, more deeply into us, and therefore seldom permits us a purely aesthetic enjoyment of it. Whereas the work that is manifestly not symbolical appeals much more vividly to our aesthetic sensibility, because it offers us an harmonious vision of fulfilment."[19]

If the attempt is made to explain the nature of the Visionary Mode's obscurity as "substitutes for . . . unacceptable experience"[20] of the author, as the Freudian method would have us do, then we are taken away "from the psychological study of the work of art" and confronted with only "the psychic disposition of the poet himself." But Jung's analysis, in respect to the psychological telos of symbolic art, has stoutly maintained that:

119

... the work of art is something in its own right, and may not be conjured away.... It is essential that we give serious consideration to the basic experience that underlies it—namely, to the vision.

From the point of view of what is called contemporary Common Sense, the tendency is to discount "a vision" as an aberration, a phenomenon which has about it the associations of "occultism." Consequently, visionary experience is *dismissed* as "the outcome of a rich fantasy or of a poetic mood—that is to say, as a kind of poetic license psychologically understood," on the principle that "it would be better not to take such things too seriously, lest the world revert again to a benighted superstition." Jung notices that even authors themselves support this commonly maintained attitude, "in order to put a wholesome distance between themselves and their work." Nevertheless, "the truth is that poets are human beings, and that what a poet says about his work is often far from being the most illuminating word on the subject. What is required of us, then, is nothing less than to defend the importance of the visionary experience against the poet himself."

In being confronted by a work in the Visionary Mode, the problem is to understand precisely what the material consists of or what it refers to.

We are astonished, taken aback, confused, put on our guard or even disgusted—and we demand commentaries and explanations. We are reminded in nothing of everyday, human life, but rather of dreams, night-time fears and the dark recesses of the

120

mind that we sometimes sense with misgivings.

Jung states that he is specifically thinking of such examples as the second part of Goethe's *Faust*, of Dante's *Comedia*, of Wagner's *Nibelungenring*, the poetry of William Blake, *The Shepherd* of Hermas, and *Moby Dick* in association with these remarks. He might equally well refer to *The Golden Ass* of Apuleius, Medieval Romances, the tragedies of Shakespeare, Cervantes' *Don Quixote*, Swift's *Gulliver's Travels*, Kafka's novels, etc. But, as he remarks, "literary products of highly dubious merit are often of the greatest interest to the psychologist," and consequently he makes reference, also, to Rider Haggard's group of novels about *She*, Benoit's *L'Atlantide*, Kubin's *Die Andere Seite*, Meyrink's *Das Grüne Gesicht*, Goetz's *Das Reich ohne Raum*, and Barlach's *Der Tote Tag*.

In every instance of an art-work in the Visionary Mode, his point is that the psychologist is confronted by the question of the psychic meaning of the material. "The visionary experience is cloaked" in Dante, for example, by historical and theological information, and in Wagner by mythology. "But with neither of them does the moving force and the deeper significance lie there." The symbolic value of *Moby Dick* is not to be comprehended as having its source in the nineteenth century conditions of whaling. But just as the sources of the visionary experience are not reducible to the historical, mythical, or intellectual "material" it employs, neither is it reducible to the personal unconscious of the creative artist. In all such reductions it would be assumed that the explanation is possible because that to which the "obscure" vision is re-

121

duced is, in fact, better known, is "clear," in which case, the visionary work of art would not remain something in its own right, but would be "conjured away."

In works of art of this nature — and we must never confuse them with the artist as a person — we cannot doubt that the vision is a genuine, primordial experience, regardless of what reason-mongers may say. The vision is not something derived or secondary, and it is not a symptom of something else. It is true symbolic expression — that is, the expression of something existent in its own right, but imperfectly known.

Even in such works as *The Shepherd* of Hermas, *The Divine Comedy*, and *Faust*, in which the reader can "catch the reverberations of an initial love-experience . . . in each of them we find the personal love episode not only connected with the weightier visionary experience, but frankly subordinated to it. On the strength of this evidence which is furnished by the work of art itself and which throws out of court the question of the poet's particular psychic disposition, we must admit that the vision represents a deeper and more impressive experience than human passion."

The love-episode is a real experience really suffered, and the same statement applies to the vision. We need not try to determine whether the content of the vision is of a physical, psychic or metaphysical nature. In itself it has psychic reality, and this is no less real than physical reality.

122

Consequently, for Jung, the essence of the problem concerning the psychological meaning of art-works in the Visionary Mode is focused on the nature of symbolism. "Through our feelings we experience the known, but our intuition points to things that are unknown and hidden — that by their very nature are secret." Thus, by introducing the general principles of his theory of individual psychology into the field of aesthetics, Jung is able to offer his answer to the question.

> The creative process, insofar as we are able to follow it at all, consists in an *unconscious animation of the archetype*, and in a development and shaping of this image till the work is completed.[21]

It should be recalled that what is meant by the collective unconscious is "a certain psychic disposition shaped by the forces of heredity ... [archetypes of which] show all the traits of primitive levels of psychic development."[22] The so-called archetype or primordial image is a figure, "whether it be a daemon, man, or process, that repeats itself in the course of history wherever creative phantasy is freely manifested. Essentially, therefore, it is a mythological figure. If we subject these images to a closer investigation, we discover them to be the formulated resultants of countless typical experiences of our ancestors. They are, as it were, the psychic residua of numberless experiences of the same type. They depict millions of individual experiences in the average, presenting a kind of picture of the psychic life distributed and projected into the manifold shapes of the mythological pandemonium."[23]

123

Just as Jung has maintained that "seers, prophets, lead-
ers and enlighteners"[24] are in touch with the contents of
the collective unconscious, and that "the most effective
ideals are always more or less transparent variants of the
archetype,"[25] so now he asserts that, while causalistic-
reductive scientific thought would have us repudiate such
a realm of psychic experience, "because of our fear of
superstition and metaphysics, and because we strive to
construct a conscious world that is safe and manageable
in that natural law holds in it the place of statute law in
a commonwealth,"[26] the contravening fact is that "the
poet now and then catches sight of the figures that people
the night-world—the spirits, demons and gods. He knows
that a purposiveness out-reaching human ends is the life-
giving secret for man; he has a presentiment of incom-
prehensibe happenings in the pleroma. In short, he sees
something of that psychic world that strikes terror into
the savage and the barbarian."

Jung, consequently, makes the interpretation that the
content of the vision "cannot have had its source in any
experience of the external world. It is rather a symbol that
stands for a psychic happening; it covers an experience
of the inner world."

It is for this reason that no theory of psychology would
be justified in pretending to "explain away" works of art
in the Visionary Mode. Jung's contention is that his analytical psychology must not be misinterpreted as doing
anything of the sort. Symbols are not "explained away"
by tracing them to sources in archetypes of the collective
unconscious, for the simple reason that the archetypes

124

are not "better known."

> These mythological forms ... are in themselves
> themes of creative phantasy that still await their
> translation into conceptual language, of which there
> exists as yet only laborious beginnings. These con-
> cepts, for the most part still to be created, could pro-
> vide us with an abstract scientific understanding of
> the unconscious processes that are the roots of the
> primordial images.[27]

In effect, the archetypes are posited as possibilities, on
the basis of precisely such finished or shaped material as
one finds in works of Visionary experience. "The shaping
of the primordial image is, as it were, a translation into
the language of the present which makes it possible for
every man to find again the deepest springs of life which
would otherwise be closed to him."

One is now in a position to see what Jung's interpretation is of the psychic significance of visionary works of
art, and of the nature of the autonomous complex in the
creative process.

> What is of particular importance for the study of
> literature in these manifestations of the collective
> unconscious is that they are *compensatory* to the
> conscious attitude. This is to say that they can bring
> a one-sided, abnormal, or dangerous state of con-
> sciousness into equilibrium in *an apparently pur-
> posive way*.[28]

And again:

125

Recoiling from the unsatisfying present the yearning of the artist reaches out to that primordial image in the unconscious which is best fitted to *compensate* the insufficiency and one-sidedness of the spirit of the age. The artist seizes this image and in the work of raising it from the deepest unconsciousness he brings it into relation with conscious values, thereby transforming its shape, until it can be accepted by his contemporaries according to their powers.[29]

The language in this last passage should not be misleading. That the metaphor is used of the artist "reaching out" and "seizing" a content of the collective unconscious is nowhere supported in Jung's writings by the implication that it lies within the conscious power or will of the artist to "choose" such content. Although the function i.e., the psychic significance of the work of art with symbolic value, is seen as compensatory to a conscious state, it cannot be "manufactured" under the conditions of conscious wish-fulfilment. Why a particular artist is possessed by such an experience of an archetype as he is able to shape into an effective work in the Visionary Mode: "cannot be fathomed,"[30] except in the sense that

Art is a kind of innate drive that seizes a human being and makes him its instrument. The artist is not a person endowed with free will who seeks his own ends, but one who allows art to realize its purposes through him. As a human being he may have moods and a will and personal aims, but as an artist he is "man" in a higher sense — he is "collective man" — one who carries and shapes the unconscious, psy-

126

chic life of mankind. To perform this difficult office it is sometimes necessary for him to sacrifice happiness and everything that makes life worth living for the ordinary human being.

Thus, Jung employed the principles and the methods of his general psychology in attempting to discover what light his science can throw on the nature of art. Taking the concept of integration, or the image of "wholeness," to stand for the psychic health of an individual, in the on-going processes of living, and applying his theory of the symbol as distinguished from the sign, Jung characterizes Visionary art as that which can be understood— if at all, i.e., to a small degree—only in connection with the assumed "purposive role" played by archetypes of the collective unconscious.

> Psychology can do nothing toward the elucidation of this colorful imagery except bring together materials for comparison and offer a terminology for its discussion.

The terminology is taken from the Jungian analysis of individual psychology. Therefore, the idea of the symbolic function derived from the analysis of patients' dreams, active imagination, drawings, etc., is extended to that of the public realm of art. Here it is not a question of formal cause (of standards of art criticism) but of final cause, namely, what *purpose* does the symbolic work of art fulfill in the psychic life of a society; what is its psychic significance? Jung believes symbolical art-work serves the same purpose for a society that an individual

127

symbolic experience serves for a patient in therapy. In-sofar as it does compensate for a social-historical one-sidedness it is, also, a "reconciling factor" and possesses, potentially, "transcending power." Whereas, in the *individual* it represents or adumbrates "a line for future development"—the *socially* significant symbol

> ... speaks with the voice of thousands and ten thousands, foretelling changes in the conscious out-look of [its] time.... Every period has its bias, its particular prejudice and its psychic ailment. An epoch is like an individual; it has its own limitations of conscious outlook, and therefore requires a com-pensatory adjustment. This is effected by the collec-tive unconscious in that a poet, a seer or a leader allows himself to be guided by the unexpressed de-sire of his times and shows the way, by word or deed, to the attainment of that which everyone blindly craves and expects—whether this attainment results in good or evil, the healing of an epoch or its de-struction.

Likewise, as the symbolic function in the individual's psychology does not have its source in the personal un-conscious, but in that of the collective, so is it with the source of Visionary art. "The primordial experience is the source of his creativeness; it cannot be fathomed, and therefore requires mythological imagery to give it form. ... It is merely a deep presentiment that strives to find expression. It is like a whirlwind that seizes everything within reach and, by carrying it aloft, assumes a visible shape." In this respect it will be seen to have the character

128

of an autonomous complex. But it does not follow that
the symbolic function, in such cases, is simply one of
compensation for the artist's own conscious one-sidedness. The question of the would-be work of art having
value for others than the one who created it is formulated as follows. "In what relation does it stand to the
conscious outlook of [its] time?"

> Great poetry draws its strength from the life of
> mankind, and we completely miss its meaning if we
> try to derive it from personal factors. Whenever the
> collective unconscious becomes a living experience
> and is brought to bear upon the conscious outlook of
> an age, this event is a creative act which is of im-
> portance to everyone living in that age. A work of
> art is produced that contains what may truthfully
> be called a message to generations of men.

In sum, then, the psychic significance of the symbolic
art work is that of "restoring the psychic equilibrium of
the epoch." In the terminology of Jung's psychology, a
work is not symptomatic or a sign but symbolic if its
origins cannot be traced to personal factors but to collective ones and if it has a prospective value.

> To grasp its meaning, we must allow it to shape
> us as it once shaped [the artist]. We see that he has
> drawn upon the healing and redeeming forces of the
> collective psyche that underlies consciousness with
> its isolation and its painful errors; that he has pene-
> trated to that matrix of life in which all men are em-
> bedded, which imparts a common rhythm to all

human existence, and allows the individual to communicate his feeling and his striving to mankind as a whole.

Thereby, Jung offers a basis for an historical analysis of psychically significant works of art. "The nature of the work of art permits conclusions to be drawn concerning the character of the period from which it sprang." [31] Consequently, a psychological interpretation can be offered in answer to such questions as: "What was the significance of realism and naturalism to their age? What was the meaning of romanticism, or Hellenism? They were tendencies of art which brought to the surface that unconscious element of which the contemporary mental atmosphere had most need. The artist as educator of his time—much could be said about that today."

In drawing the parellel between individual and social psychology, Jung is saying that the two cases are alike in the reason why "eruptions" from the collective unconscious occur, and in the possibilities for improvement which such developments make available.

> The struggle of adaptation is laborious, because we have constantly to be dealing with individual, i.e., atypical conditions. No wonder then, that at the moment when a typical situation occurs, we feel suddenly aware of an extraordinary release, as though transported, or caught up as by an overwhelming power. At such moments we are no longer individuals, but the race; the voice of all mankind resounds in us.

It is for this reason that every relation to material which has its source in the archetypes is felt to be " 'stirring', i.e., it is impressive, it calls up a stronger voice than our own. The man who speaks with primordial images ... transmutes personal destiny into the destiny of mankind, thus evoking all those beneficient forces that have enabled mankind to find a rescue from every hazard and to outlive the longest night."

> Therein lies the social importance of art; it is constantly at work educating the spirit of the age, since it brings to birth those forms in which the age is most lacking. ... [Art] represents a process of mental self-regulation in the life of nations and epochs.

SECTION 5: *The Literary Artist*

While Jung has made his argument that the psychic significance of symbolical works of art is analogous to that of the individual symbol for a patient in psychotherapy, it is clear that he has left unexamined the psychological meaning of non-symbolic art-works, a question we must turn to in the next chapter. But it would be well here to summarize the concluding remarks on which Jung's interpretation of the artist rests.

The creator of symbolic, imaginative, works in the Visionary Mode seems to be an "unbalanced" person. The way in which he is "different" from the normal man, and the relation between such difference and his role as a means by which correctives can be offered in his art,

131

compensatory to his age, are described metaphorically by Jung in the following way.

While the normal man is the one adapted to, or at least able to endure, the one-sidedness peculiar to his age, "the man who takes to the by-streets and alley-ways because, unlike the normal man, he cannot endure the broad highway, will be the first to discover those elements that lie apart from the main streets, and that await a new participation in life. The artist's relative lack of adaptation becomes his real advantage; for it enables him to keep aloof from the high-ways, the better to follow his own yearning and to find those things which the others are deprived of without noticing it."

It should be remembered that Jung makes no attempt to answer the question of why any given man (a) becomes different from the "normal," or (b) expresses his creativity as an artist rather than as a "seer, prophet, leader or enlightener." Jung has not made an analysis of the artist as a person; rather his concern has been with the psychological interpretation of art itself. "In his capacity of artist [the person] . . . is objective and impersonal— even inhuman—for *as an artist* he *is* his *work*, and not a human being." [32] Since Jung conceives of every *creative* person as a "duality or a synthesis of contradictory aptitudes," on one side he is a human being with a personal life, "while on the other side he is an impersonal creative process."

A statement like this, after all, only points up the fact that psychology is not a unified science, and that the concept of "person" and "personal life" is still wide open to interpretation, as is the correlative concept of "imper-

132

sonality." To speak of a human being *qua* artist as impersonal makes sense within the Jungian system because it reflects the entire structure of his general psychology.

Jung is perfectly willing to make the distinction between a human being as a person whose psychology may be "sound or morbid," ascertainable by analysis of "his psychic make-up to find the determinants of his personality," on the one hand; but insists that, on the other hand, "we can understand him in his capacity of artist only by looking at his creative achievement." That is, *not* by trying to explain the creative achievement in terms of his personal psychology. This is why:

> The personal life of the poet cannot be held essential to his art—but at most a help or a hindrance to his creative task. He may go the way of a Philistine, a good citizen, a neurotic, a fool or a criminal. His personal career may be inevitable and interesting, but it does not explain the poet.

In other words, the term "artist" does not designate a specific type or class of psychological nature, such as the term "psychotic" or "neurotic" does; rather, it is the name of a class of people determined a posteriori, on the basis of their creative accomplishments. In this it is closer to such class designations as "English gentleman" or "Prussian officer." And "we should make a sad mistake if we tried to explain the mode of life of an English gentleman, a Prussian officer or a cardinal in terms of personal factors. The gentleman, the officer and the cleric function *as such* in an *impersonal* role, and their psychic make-up is qualified by a peculiar *objectivity*."[33]

We must grant that the artist does not function in an official capacity—the very opposite is nearer the truth. He nevertheless resembles the type I have named in one respect, for the specifically artistic disposition involves an overweight of collective psychic life as against the personal.[34]

This is only a way of saying that the term "artist" names a phenomenological category which is irreducible; not to be explained by "tracing" the sources of the activity of the artist to his personal life. Although the one who is an artist is identified as such because he has been able to "shape" the unconscious psychic life of mankind, *why* it is that anyone should have such powers (*to give shape to* content of the collective unconscious which erupt in him) remains a mystery that can be referred to only with such a metaphor as "a gift"—a symbol, that, after all, implies a value which is not earned but comes to one gratuitously.

The life of an artist is, often, unsatisfactory. But this Jung explains as a consequence of the conflict that expresses the two contrary forces at play within him: "the common human longing for happiness, satisfaction and security in life, and . . . a ruthless passion for creation which may go so far as to override every personal desire." The *passion for creation* is not to be explained away. It is referred to as "the divine gift of the creative fire," and again as "a special ability" which imposes its own "task."

The lives of artists are as a rule unsatisfactory— not to say tragic—because of their inferiority on the human and personal side, and not because of a sinister

134

dispensation. There is hardly any exception to the rule that a person must pay dearly for the divine gift of creative fire.... A special ability means a heavy expenditure of energy in a particular direction, with a consequent drain from some other side of life.

The secret of artistic creation and of the effectiveness of art is to be found in a return to the state of *participation mystique*—to that level of experience at which it is man who lives, and not the individual, and at which the weal and woe of the single human being does not count, but only human existence. This is why every great work of art is objective and impersonal, but none the less profoundly moves us each and all.

Therefore, to attempt to explain art-works in terms of the pre-conditions in the psychic economy of the artist, is a blind alley of would-be scientific thought for no reason so much as the fact that it would be based on a theory of psychology inadequate for the comprehension of the final cause—the psychic significance—of art itself. "The work in process becomes the poet's fate and determines his psychic development," not the other way around.

It makes no difference whether the poet knows that his work is begotten, grows or matures with him, or whether he supposes that by taking thought he produces it out of the void. His opinion of the matter does not change the fact that his own work outgrows him as a child its mother.

135

PART
III

Conclusions
and Criticisms

There is a multitude of problems concerned with the possibility of making a judgment on the soundness and usefulness of Jung's ideas. The foregoing chapters, dealing with Jung's psychology in general, his theory of symbolism in particular, and the implications he draws from these for aesthetics, on the whole have presented his ideas in his own words, with a minimum of critical digressions, despite the fact that they have been structured by me and, in various contexts, expanded for purposes of clarity. This has resulted in the concluding chapter standing now like the silent witness who suddenly asks at the end of a presentation, "But it is *true?*"

A variety of questions must be considered. My intention is to examine them under the following headings:

(1) Questions concerning Jung's general psychology in relation, especially, to the problem of the archetypes of the collective unconscious, namely, *Cultural Universals and the Archetypes*. (2) Questions concerning Jung's stated and undrawn implications for the study of art, namely, *Jungian Psychology and Aesthetics*. And (3) questions concerning the implications of Jung's theories for the problems of knowledge, namely, *Symbolism and Epistemology*.

SECTION I: *Cultural Universals and the Archetypes*

It is not within the province of philosophical criticsm to determine the scientific validity of Jungian psychology, except insofar as philosophy of science stipulates criteria for what is acceptable as scientific in general. In effect, philosophy of science is characterized by its examination of epistemological method, and the ways in which scientists present their arguments. It is primarily concerned with the validity of implications drawn by scientists, rather than with specifications for the subject matters of such research, discovery, and theory.

Some of the most glaring difficulties that Jung's psychology presents to philosophic analysis are based on the fact that many of his implications are stated in metaphoric rather than literal language. That the structure of his psychology as a whole would meet the over-all demands for science — that it does unify special assumptions under more general ones, that it does indicate its own tests for validation of specific hypotheses, and that it does facilitate the formulation of new hypotheses which in turn can

SECTION 1: *Cultural Universals and the Archetypes*

be tested by its methods—all that notwithstanding, the fact appears that to an "outsider" the most difficult problem would be to identify and explain the nature of his subject matter. That is, not only the hypothesis of "unconsciousness," but the uniquely Jungian construct of such a subject matter as he calls the *Collective Unconscious.*

The unconscious cannot be an object of any possible direct scientific inquiry. All statements about such a hypothetical subject matter depend on assumptions drawn from certain types of conscious experience. For example, in Freud's writing one finds the statement that "an instinct can never be an object of consciousness—only the idea that represents the instinct."[1] Likewise, in Jung's writing there is the statement that the whole structure of an analytical psychology is "a provisional one" depending on whether "the hypothesis of the unconscious holds true, which in turn can only be verified if unconscious contents can be changed into conscious ones—if . . . the disturbance emanating from the unconscious . . . can successfully be integrated into consciousness by the interpretative method."[2]

Nevertheless, problems of unconsciousness-in-general aside, there is a special problem in recognizing the idea of a Collective Unconscious as a legitimate subject matter for the science of psychology. It is in this connection that the metaphoric language is which Jung presents his hypothesis offers the greatest obstacles. From the ageless controversies over whether causal or functional elements in human psychology are inherited or derived from the environment, a continuation of the debate seems to be carried, now, into questions of the unconscious, as well. For

141

Freud, it appears that the unconscious is constituted of (1) inherited instinctual drives (the impersonal, the Id), (2) the unconscious aspects of Ego, and (3) an unconscious functional system derived from the environment (the individual's Super-Ego). Whereas for Jung, by comparison, it appears that he considers both Freud's Id and his Super-Ego as the contents of the Personal Unconscious, placing special emphasis on the theory that most of such contents are derived environmentally; moreover, Jung supplements the concept with a relatively even greater content that is impersonal and inherited, but not of the nature of instintual drives, namely, the Collective Unconscious. The metaphorical language, of which I spoke, is employed in order to give what "evidence" Jung offers to substantiate the method of inheritance, as well as to characterize the contents. They are described as having a "mythological character"; at the same time Jung uses analogies drawn from physics and technology, in order to speak of how the representations of such content function. They are spoken of as *analogous with* river-beds, etc.; and the symbols of such primordial images or archetypes function *like* (1) siphons, and, more importantly, *like* (2) transformers. But, at this point, it should be clear that the greatest difficulty is with the argument by which Jung believes the inheritance and possible cumulative changes of the Collective Unconscious may be brought about. The root question is, How can the Collective Unconscious be transmitted?

Jung offers his "evidence" by anology. "In the physical structure of the body," he writes, "we find traces of earlier stages of evolution, and we may expect the human psyche also to conform in its make-up to the law of phylogeny."[3] But what support does he have for this "expectation"? The biologists who are concerned with explaining the mechanism by which physical factors are inherited do so by means of the content and function of genes. And there is considerable doubt among contemporary biologists and geneticists as to whether any genetic medium whatsoever may be discovered which would justify the belief in the inheritability of acquired characteristics. But Jung conceives of the archetypes of the Collective Unconscious, precisely, as the "residue" — another analogy — of countless hundreds of thousands of "typical" human, and even possibly, animal, experiences; as "acquired characteristics" of reaction, i.e., typical *ways* of apprehension, of feeling, and of thought. Not inherited ideas, but inherited *dispositions* for certain ways of intuiting, feeling, and thinking.

Jung appeals only to the ideas of the biologist Semon, who employs the concept of "engrams" — which Jung interprets as "imprints" that "through the condensation of innumerable, similar processes"[4] of mnemic deposits, contribute to the change of the very brain structure.

> ... The uncertainty of our speculation has been greatly increased by the necessity for borrowing from the science of biology. Biology is truly a land of unlimited possibilities. We may expect it to give us the most surprising information and we cannot guess what answers it will return in a few years[5] to the questions we have put to it. They may be of a kind which will blow away the whole of our artificial

structure of hypotheses.[6]

It is curious to note that the statement above is quoted from a passage in which Freud puts into doubt the possible soundness of his hypothesis of a death instinct. All the more true is it of Jung—insofar as his Collective Unconscious is conceived to be transmitted exclusively in the biological constituents of inheritance. Contemporary biology does not support the idea of the inheritance of any acquired characteristics. Does this vitiate Jung's hypothesis of a Collective Unconscious? It does—to the extent that Jung's position is left without an essential element: a means for biological transmission.

But does the unacceptability to contemporary genetics of the idea of inheritable "imprints" of archaic psychic life do away with the questions to answer which Jung posited the Collective Unconscious?

Clearly, the answer is that it does not. The problem is this: how is it possible to explain such psychic phenomena —i.e., specific psychic content—as cannot be traced to environmental experiences or instinctual drives of a biological nature? Apparently, the most informative features of such phenomena is, first, their similarity, universally, regardless of cultural differences, and second, the fact that they are typified as symbolic—especially in reference to their function in religious and aesthetic systems. I wish to indicate the manner in which Freud himself, and then certain anthropologists, handle this problem.

The only Freudian analyst and theoretician who has written an extensive study of the psychology of C. G. Jung is the British Doctor, Edward Glover. His book[7] is a dogmatic and vitriolic attack. Jung is, for him, a renegade Freudian who is foisting obfuscation on the unwary. His major thesis is that Jung offers only "a drawing-room version of psychic development" [8]; that is, "Jung reveals himself in his true colors as a conventional almost academic conscious psychologist." [9]

Glover's critical comparison itself can hardly be held up as a model of cogent thinking, since it presents an extraordinary collection of unexamined assumptions, incomplete arguments, and *non sequitur* conclusions; but it will be informative to see how he handles the difference between Freud and Jung in respect to the contents of the Collective Unconscious, and the nature of symbolism.

> The idea that in psychic as in somatic affairs ontogeny repeats in blurred outline the story of phylogeny has stimulated many psychologists. Its application to psychic affairs calls, however, for the closest discipline; and, other things being equal, preference should be given to explanations in terms of individual development. [10]

Now, of course, it is Jung's position that the "other things" are not "equal," i.e., that the phenomena cannot be as informatively interpreted semiotically as symbolically.

Glover suggests that, in order to account for the process of symbol formation, one should study the primitive thinking process of the child. He grants, however, that the "primary process" *cannot* be observed directly; it is inferred. But, by his interpretation, "what the adult regards as a peculiar form of symbolism is to the child a matter of fact."[11] That he argues only on the basis of "probability" gives him reason to regard it as more "likely" that the content of all such symbolism has as its referents actual experiences in the individual's development. The inference is, apparently, based on nothing more than the prejudice in favor of "environment" as against "heredity," as the tool of explanation with "economy" of hypotheses.

> It may be said not only that many [sic] Jungian archetypes are capable of adequate explanation in terms of purely individual thought but also that so long as we have not fully explored the early forms of individual thinking, the validity and universality of the collective archetype is under strong suspicion.

Obviously, the qualification "many" is a loophole. Glover is forced to recognize and admit it is arguable that "inherited psychic predispositions express themselves through whatever form of individual organization may have developed." The simple fact is that Freud himself writes: "The content of the unconscious is in any case collective, a general possession of mankind." The essential difference is that Freud wishes to describe the content of the unconscious in biological terms exclusively and objects to there being any content described mythologically. That is what he *wishes* to do, at least; what he actually does is another story.

When Freud is writing of religious phenomena, for example, he takes the position that "in the absence of individual traumatic expriences these . . . can be understood only phylogenetically."

In *Moses and Monotheism* (1939) ... he asserted that "the archaic heritage of mankind includes not only archaic dispositions but also ideational contents, memory traces of the experiences of former generations." Freud realized fully that the present attitude of biological science rejects the idea of acquired qualities being transmitted to descendents. Nothing daunted by this opposition, he maintained that he was unable to picture biological development without taking this into account.

It is a quaint thing to see how, when Freud maintains these ideas in opposition to the present state of biology he is, for Glover, the "undaunted," "objective" pioneer, but when Jung maintains such ideas he is a "reactionary." The same is true (in Kris as in Glover) concerning changes made in their theoretical constructions. When Freud revises, alters, reformulates, he is "true to the conditions of on-going scientific thinking," he is "realistic"; but when Jung revises, because his concepts appear to be "in a state of flux," he is "mystifying."

The point is quite simple. Like Jung, Freud also requires for psychological explanation a hypothetically inheritable collective psyche, particularly in order to deal with public symbolic systems. When Glover summarizes this position, he simply begs all of the important questions.

We can neither prove nor disprove the inheritance of psychic memory traces. All we can say is that with increasing understanding ... of the mental function of two-year olds we shall in all probability find that many apparently unreasonable infantile reactions are amply accounted for without assuming more than the inheritance of instinctual dispositions, of sensitiveness of psychic reaction and of thought dispositions.

The whole issue, apparently, turns on whether such dispositions and "sensitiveness" can be adequately conceived in biological terms or not. For a psychologist to maintain that "unreasonable" reactions would *probably* be "accounted for" by the inheritance of such "dispositions" is to say that they can*not* be accounted for in a causally-reductive system. It is the "scientific" equivalent of saying, in common parlance, that certain people are born with "talent," or the equivalent, as we shall see, of the concept of "genius," which anthropologists make use of.

Despite his affirmation of the above position, Glover maintains categorically that "there is *no resemblance* between" Freud's idea of phylogenetic traces in psychic life and the "representations of the Collective Unconscious described by Jung as archetypes." The difference, of course, turns on the interpretation of symbolism.

Freud drew an analogy between individual neurotic symptom formation and the phenomena of "mass psychology," e.g., in religion, and correlated both of them with "traumatic events occurring in the primeval history of man . . . consonant with his own theories of individual mental development and function."

> Freud maintained that the inherited phylogenetic fragments referred only to events of catastrophic (traumatic) significance occurring in primeval times

and concerned, not with allegorical abstractions, but with the concrete development of the human family.[12]

It may very well be that Glover simply will not read Jung accurately enough to recognize that he does not conceive the referents of the archetypes to be allegorical abstractions (it is the typical events of archaic life to which they refer), so that he may be forgiven this misrepresentation. But, it seems to be that, nothing other than intellectual naivete can explain Glover's belief that Freud's characterizations of the catastrophic events of primeval times are themselves other than allegorical abstractions. It is perfectly clear that the single traumatic event with which Freud was concerned in this context was the murder of the Father by his Sons, "a combination of sexual and aggressive elements," which does not have its roots in "concrete" (sic!) history but in Freudian psychology, pure and simple. The obvious fact is that Freud has *not* gone from what is "better known" in history to explain something in individual psychology. He has simply projected into "primeval times" the conditions which he discovered giving rise to neuroses. For Freud, "primeval" history is an allegory of "the family romance." But then *all* symbolic manifestations of the human psyche are parables of the individual's unconscious conflicts, or struggles between consciousness and the unconscious. That is to say, they can be interpreted in terms of individual mental functions and development. In sum, we can learn nothing new from symbols; rather, we are able to interpret symbols because we already know what

149

functions they serve in individual psychic life.

Consequently, Glover is able to announce dogmatically that "the conditions giving rise to symbol formation are strictly limited. Although the number of symbols runs into thousands, the *unconscious ideas represented* in symbols are confined to a small number of *primitive interests* concerning the subject's own body, family figures, and the phenomena of birth, sexuality, and death."[13] We can learn nothing new from symbols not only because there is no " 'higher' idea implicit in the symbolism [but, moreover, because] the unconscious derivatives present in the symbol formation act as an obstacle to the development of more realistic representations." The prejudice is perfectly clear: granted that (according to Glover) science is not conceived as having any symbolic function, what is conventionally taken to be symbolic in art or religion is necessarily an obstacle to "realistic" conception for the simple reason that only science offers us such "realism."

Despite the fact that Freud agrees with the latter conditions for explanation, and therefore would remain in opposition to Jung's interpretation of symbolism, he did argue for the inheritance of acquired characteristics of a limited kind. Glover wants to have it both ways. He is compelled to state Freud's own position on this point, but he declares, "many Freudian analysts prefer to think, symbols are recreated in the course of individual development," "whether Freud's view that symbols represent phylogenetic traces is accurate," or not. Better still is Glover's over-all conclusion on this point. "The whole structure of Freudian metapsychology is unaffected by his incursion into the region of phylogenetic speculation."

Whether this bespeaks inconsistency, or is due to the late development of these concerns of Freud and are, therefore, insufficiently integrated into his system of psychology, Glover does not even attempt to answer.

Nevertheless, it is Glover's summary judgment that Jung's "witting on unwitting policy" is to level "distinctions between the unconscious and the conscious," which, *"confuses archetypes with traditions."*[14] In other words, in spite of all of his own qualifications, Glover holds to the idea that the so-called contents of the Collective Unconscious are, actually, derived from the individual's cultural environment. That cultures are different —and, therefore, offer different "traditions"—contributes nothing to the question of why there are *similarities* among symbolic manifestations, *despite* cultural differences. It is the "Freudian" assumption that similarities are to be explained by the universality of "the family romance."

One imagines that if one appeals to anthropolgists he will find the question, perhaps, answered somewhat differently. It might be assumed that their comparative studies would throw light on the problem of found similarities among symbolic manifestations. But one is surprised to discover that anthropolgists, generally speaking, are not interested in such specfic manifestations, ". . . for the study of many cultures had taught them that no specific form of any institution has universal scope."[15] It is types, or classes of "traditions," i.e., it is "institutions" as such, and not their *specific manifestations*, with which the anthropologist concerns himself. That this is an abstraction, and often an hypostatized one, the sophisticated anthropologist is aware. Nevertheless, when such a re-searcher tries to formulate a theoretical structure for his comparative studies, he formulates the "universals" in human civilization in terms of "institutions."

The very distinguished Professor Herskovits has made a survey of the formulations of culture universals that have been attempted during the past eighty years.[16] In 1881, E. B. Tylor characterized cultural universals in the following categories: language; the "arts of life" (eco-nomics, commerce, etc.); the "arts of pleasure" (poetry, the plastic arts, etc.); science; religion; history and myth-ology; and "society" or social institutions. C. Wissler, in 1923, reformulated the list under the following headings: speech; material traits (food habits, dress, etc.); art; mythology and scientific knowledge; religious practices; family and social systems; property; government; and war. The logical conclusion of this sort of schematization has been achieved by G. P. Murdock, 1945, in his *Com-mon Denominator of Cultures*, and *Outline of Cultural Materials*, in which he divides culturally universal tra-ditions into forty-six categories, alphabetically, from "age-grading" through "calendar, cleanliness training, etc.," to "weather control," each of which is sub-divided and cross-referenced. But the question to ask is whether such descriptive typologies tell us anything about why there are such abstract similarities.

One of the earliest postulates of anthropological science was that the *ends* achieved by all human cultures are basically similar. This universality in the general outlines of cultures supported the theory of

152

the *"psychic unity* of mankind," which held that the resemblances between the institutions of different cultures are to be accounted for by the similar *capacities* of all men.[17]

Since the days of Herbert Spencer, anthropologists have tried to distinguish between "basic needs" — taken to be universal, and "cultural responses" — viewed as culturally distinguishable by content, but formally universal. Wissler offers a biological interpretation of cultural universals. He believed that man's nature is "as fixed as that of any social insect" and contains a *drive* to build cultures, conditioned by his early learning process. The universals are a result of inborn responses; the variants depend on different childhood conditioning. Herskovits comments that "a genetic basis for culture implies a genetic mechanism; and this has never been discovered."

Malinowski employs a list of seven "basic needs" to account for the universality of cultural institutions, namely, metabolism; reproduction; bodily comforts; safety; movement; growth; health. The cultural responses to these "basic needs" determine a series of "derived needs." The latter are imposed upon every child in any culture, through the process of learning. These "derived needs" are characterized by Malinowski as (1) economics; (2) social control; (3) education; and (4) political organization. "We are struck," Herskovits writes, "with the omission of any reference to religion or the aesthetic elements of culture. Is the universality of these aspects less securely established than are the domains of economics or social organization?" Actually, Malinowski does go on to say that, besides satisfying man's biological needs, there are cultural "responses" such as "creative and artistic expression." But, Herskovits points out, "what *needs* are satisfied by these . . . we are not told."

G. P. Murdock considers that only a small proportion of man's action springs directly from "any of the demonstrable basic drives," and therefore adds *habit formation* as a principle of explanation equal in importance with that of *instinct*. But this seems only to repeat the pattern of anthropological thinking—from biologically determined "basic needs" to geographically and chronologically variable "derived needs"—without adding any concept of value for interpretation.

Herskovitz is discontent with all such schematizations, and judges that, while they are useful descriptions, they do not offer principles for analysis. Insofar as cultural universals are concerned, if one tries to explain them in respect to "basic needs" then anthropology must yield to biology, whereas, if one tries to concentrate on the variable, "derived needs" then anthropology must yield to history.

In any event, he points out that "concerning the origin and development of culture . . . we have no information." He assumes it to be incontrovertible that there are biological bases for "the behavior of individuals that fashion culture." But to infer from this that *all* cultural activity is derived from and reducible to the biological bases "tends to lead us into rationalizations rather than explanations that are today scientifically verifiable." Evidently, the principle is—no known genetic mechanism, therefore, no scientific (causally-reductive) knowledge.

To the question which Boas had put to anthropology of why the *contents* of all cultures might be referred to by "a cultural morphology . . . founded on comparative studies of similar forms in different parts of the world?" Herskovits has no answer. He can only "accept the insights" which each of the above positions offers, but not accept any one of them fully because of the "incompleteness" of each. "We may here leave the question [unanswered] of why there are universal aspects in culture." But as soon as he says this, he adds categorically:

> There can be no doubt that, viewed in the large, culture does fulfil the needs of man, psychic no less than biological; that it solves for him problems whose solution is demanded both by the character of his bio-psychological make-up and the need to meet the demands of his habitat.

Is this statement not a metaphoric one, which not only reifies "culture" but ignores the possibility that culture creates as many problems as it solves? But the question at hand is whether cultural universals, as an anthropological category, can throw any light on Jung's idea of the universality of the Collective Unconscious. Is seems to me that it cannot. First, because anthropology has not offered comparative studies interpretive of similar contents of expressions found in different cultures, but concentrated on abstracted forms designated as institutions or traditions. Second, the universality of such institutions itself stands in need of explanation—which anthropology, apparently, cannot offer, and which causes it to appeal to biology (to explain organic needs) and to psychology (to explain "psychic needs"). In effect, even when it considers the universality of certain institutions, anthropology is descriptive and not analytic.

A similar situation confronts us when we ask what anthropology can tell us about art in general, or about symbolism in particular.

Herskovits states that the logic of ordering typical studies in anthropology in the generally accepted way derives from the fact that they proceed from considering those "aspects that supply the physical wants of man, to those that order social relations, and finally to the aspect which, in giving meaning to the universe, sanction everyday living, and in their aesthetic manifestations afford men some of the deepest satisfactions they experience."

While his point here is that "material culture" must not be regarded as distinct from "the nonmaterial aspects of civilization," the fact remains that this ordering of such studies is justified by only "their utility" (I assume he means facility based on habit) and is not to be mistaken for an arrangement tacitly reflective of causal relations. What the causal relations are between sculpture and the development of carving tools, for example, i.e., the relations between developments in art and developments in technology, in a given culture, are occasionally studied by anthropologists. Besides examining interrelations between these "aspects" of culture, the anthropologist does write about the arts. Herskovits, for instance, typifies the anthropologist's concern with the degree of integration of the arts with "everyday" life in nonliterate cultures as contrasted with more sophisticated ones; the developments in the arts affording evidence of cultural change; the role of cross-cultural influences; and the influence of habitat and utility on the forms of art-works. But from all this, is the anthropologist able to throw any light on the nature of art in general?

> The universality of the drive to embellish useful objects, often so elaborately that the utility of an implement is lessened in the process, has posed questions that seriously embarrass those who have interpreted human experience in strict rationalistic terms.[18]

Most of the judgments and most of the questions that anthropologists make and which their statements raise about art are implicit in this sentence. The anthropologist assumes "that the search for beauty is a universal in human experience." He characterizes this "search" as caused by an innate "aesthetic drive." He has no finer distinctions to use for characterizing "masterworks," as against what everybody else in the culture makes of the same sort, than that of "genius"—a label that is read *ex post facto* into the creator of the superior creation. ". . . The aesthetic conventions of a people . . . find realization in the *genius* of the individuals who decorate the pot, or paint the wall, or carve the statuette."

The entire treatment of the arts is descriptive, not analytic. That the creative process springs from "the play of the creative imagination" and achieves "some of the deepest satisfactions"—are the clichés which substitute for principles. They are used, not examined. What is accomplished by such comparative studies as anthropologists make are descriptions of historical changes in style, and assertions about the art-works being expressive of a "way of life." The attempt at definition, or of interpretation of psychic significance, results in generalizations such as the following.

> In the widest sense, then, art is to be thought of as any embellishment of ordinary living that is achieved with competence and has describable form.... Any manifestation of the impulse to make more beautiful and thus to heighten the pleasure of any phase of living that is so recognized by a people, must be accepted by the student of culture as aesthetically valid, and is, in consequence, to be given the designation "art."[19]

Likewise, the nature of symbolism is not illuminated by the anthropologist; it is used, as if understood, mostly (in Jung's sense) semiotically. Just as the discussion of art leaves questions of "beauty," "drive," "imagination," "satisfaction," and "utility" to the biologist, the psychologist, the economist, and the philosopher, so the use of "symbol" assumes previous comprehension.

> Human behavior, indeed, has been defined as "symbolic behavior." Working back from this factor of symbolism, then, it is apparent that by the use of symbols man gives meaning to his life. Through this he culturally defines his experience....[20]

Jung's conception of Visionary art is not so much that it defines experience as that it enables either the artist or the audience to reckon with, confront, encounter something new in experience. Without this much subtlety of thought the anthropologist does not know how to interpret the information he has, even when his data is entirely accurate. He can offer only such descriptive-historical statements as: "It could be argued ... that a meaningless form, once produced, had meaning read into it, and that there then ensued a growing competence in the realistic portrayal of the form suggested by the lines of the meaningless design."

The anthropologist posseses a wealth of data about which Jung's speculations are made. For the Jungian thesis to be tested for anything like universal validity, the anthropologist's work is indispensable. But if one suggests, as does Glover, for example, that Jung has leveled down the distinction between the unconscious and consciousness, and "built" the contents of tradition "into" psychic life, independent of empirical conditioning, confusing anthropology with psychology, then one neither appreciates the inability of anthropology to explain the universality of abstract institutions or the occurrence of similar contents in different cultures, nor the possibility which Jung does suggest for doing so. It is no more true to say that Jung's psychology is a mis-named anthropology than it is to say that anthropology cannot be improved by a more adequate theory of psychic life.

In the bio-psychological argument over the relative influence of heredity and environment in shaping cultural contents, it might have been hoped that anthropology could offer a *tertium quid* between the Freudian and Jungian positions. It might have been hoped that the category of "cultural universals," which includes Art, could show us why certain manifestations in the arts are so often found, despite differences in cultures, that they

159

might be mistaken for psychic dispositions contained in a hypothetical Collective Unconscious. But, it appears that anthropology offers no such theory. It is descriptive, not analytic; and it is has not confronted the question of similarities-despite-differences without leaning on biology and psychology.

One can come only to the following conclusion. (1) If there are such phenomena as symbols which do have prospective value (as Jung interprets this), and (2) if the referents of such symbolic content cannot be traced (reduced) to either instinctual biological drives or environmental conditioning (or relations between those two), (3) then, Jung's hypothesis of the source of such contents in a universally inheritable Collective Unconscious is as good, or as poor, a speculative suggestion for explanation as we have—in spite of the glaring drawback that, from contemporary genetics, we have no reason to believe in the genetic transmissability of such acquired characteristics. The value of any hypothesis depends on the usefulness to which it can be put. Freud himself saw the usefulness of such a hypothesis to explain phenomena which he believed his psychological system did not encompass. This is not to imply that, in his last years, Freud accepted Jung's general structure for a theory of psychology; the essence of the contrast between them rests on their different interpretations of symbolism.

SECTION 2: *Jungian Psychology and Aesthetics*

It may well be asked whether Jung has not misrepresented Freud's views on art. Certainly, it might be easy to do so, since Freud's writings directly on the subject are brief, and scattered—written at different times in his career, corresponding to certain changes in his developing theoretical structure for a general psychology. Nevertheless, it seems to me that the arguments offered in accusation of Jung "misrepresenting" Freud are made in contexts where writers are required to defend Freud against "misrepresenting" himself, too. In such summary or critical writings on the subject as one finds, for example, in Kaplan,[21], Trilling,[22] and Marcuse,[23] it is evident that Freud's analysis of creativity, in spheres other than that of art, is put in opposition to Freud's own statements about art. Kaplan, for example, writes "by *implication*, if not in explicit detail, Freud allows to art a role far more important than a passing release for the artist and a way of passing time for the onlooker."[24] Or again, Trilling, more strikingly, writes, "it is possible to say of Freud that he *ultimately* did more for our understanding of art than any other writer since Aristotle; and this being so, it can only be surprising that in his early work he should have made the *error* of treating the artist as a neurotic who escapes from reality by means of 'substitute gratifications'."[25] It is an open question which of such critics are representing Freud accurately, and which are using Freud's suggestions, from concerns other than those of art, to cultivate their own independent implications.

If one reads Freud himself, from his early (1908) essay called "The Relation of the Poet to Daydreaming," through his study of Jensen's *Gradiva*, and his biographical sketches of Leonardo, Goethe, and Dostoevsky, his essay on the "theme" of the three caskets, and on the

Moses of Michelangelo, to his late writings such as *The Future of an Illusion* as well as *Civilization and Its Discontents* (1930), one finds that Freud remains consistent with his earliest formulations of the questions which a psychoanalyst can ask concerning art-works, and the methods by which he might hope to answer them.

Freud is concerned with finding the source of creative art by considering the origin of the material which the artist transforms, the effect is has upon him, and the effect it has upon his audience. That is to say, he attempts to understand the creative process in terms of his general psychology. And he does so by what would be called "biographical means."[26]

In one of his earliest formulations he, therefore, states the hypothesis that "imaginative creation, like daydreaming, is a continuation of and substitute for the play of children."[27] As for the methods of such imaginative creation: "the writer softens the egoistical character of the daydream by changes and disguises, and he bribes us by the offer of a purely formal, that is aesthetic, pleasure in presentation of his phantasies."[28] But, of course, this is only a means of seducing the aduience; the psychological effect is the "writer's putting us into a position in which we can enjoy our own daydreams without reproach or shame."[29]

When Freud speaks of art from the point of view of the creative process in the artist, he considers that art arose as a substitute for instinct-gratification which "protects" men against the painful transition from the pleasure principle to the reality principle. It is not clear whether this is identical with saying that artistic activity functions in the same way as neurosis. Marcuse's interpretation is that: "The artist's place is . . . a realm between what Freud called 'wish-denying reality' and the 'wish-fulfilling world of fantasy'—in other words, between the bitterness of daily existence and the even more bitter realm of delusion."[30]

But when Freud speaks of art from the point of view of the audience, the sense in which it "protects" is quite clearly understood to be an illusion — a harmless, but not very helpful, illusion. The reason which explains art is seen in the interpretation that, "art offers substitute gratifications for the oldest cultural renunciations, still always most deeply felt, and for that reason serves like nothing else to reconcile men to the sacrifices they have made on culture's behalf."[31] The means by which this is achieved is that "works of art promote the feelings of identification, of which every cultural group has so much need, in the occasion they provide for the sharing of highly valued emotional experiences. And when they represent the achievements of a particular culture, thus in an impressive way recalling it to its ideals, they also subserve a narcissistic gratification."[32]

> Life as we find it is too hard for use. . . . We cannot do without palliative remedies. . . . The substitute gratifications, such as art offers, are illusions in contrast to reality, but none the less satisfying to the mind on that account, thanks to the place which phantasy has reserved for herself in mental life.[33]

In the light of this survey of Freud's conception of the relation that psychology can have with art, it seems to me inaccurate to say Jung has misinterpreted Freud, and is attacking a straw man.

Even a book published as recently as 1952, in which a contemporary Freudian analyst, Ernst Kris, considers what are *Psychoanalytic Explorations in Art*, his formulations and conclusions exactly parallel those of Freud stated above. He asks, "What are those things *like* ... which the word ART conveys? What must the men have been *like* who made these things, and what did their work mean to themselves and to their public?"[34] He conceives the relation between psychology and art-works as a form of imaginative archaeology in which the diggers are looking for the elements of the "foundation" in the individual artist's unconscious conflicts. And he specifically castigates Jung for his alleged disregard for inquiry into the "reality — the particular immediate problems of the artist and the stage of technical development of his medium— which determine in one way or another his mode of expression." But Kris announces that he himself is not concerned with the formative process by which the unconscious content is actually transformed into a work of art. "In the work of art, as in the dream, unconscious contents are alive; here too, evidences of the primary process are conspicuous, but the ego maintains its control over them, elaborates them in its own right, and sees to it that ... distortion does not go too far. 'One would like to know more about how, precisely, the ego achieves this' (Freud) but this question lies already beyond the scope of our topic. ..."

The truth is that, while none of the Freudians is particularly interested in this aspect of the problem, neither is Jung. But the Freudians put off "research into" the formative process in order to take the leap from the finished product down into the particular archaeological hole it appears to open up into the unconscious of the individual artist, and to begin their reconstruction work, from that angle, of the "meaning" the work has for the artist's individual psychology. The program this suggests is either that psychology implies the necessity for psychoanalysts becoming our critics of the arts, or that critics go to school under the analysts. In either event, this implication ignores, or forgets, the analysts' assumption that there is a sphere of criticism appropriate to what they call "formal aesthetics" [35] — and that what Freud had contrasted as "professional and technical" (the formative process) with "the content" *is*, in fine, "the *art* in the artwork." [36]

The essential problem is one of determining the exact subject matter *in a work of art* on which the analytic psychologist intends to throw light.

Both Jung and Freud assume that it is *not* "the laws of formal aesthetics" — a sphere either independently given, or presumed to be studied by philosophers of art, psychologists of consciousness, or critical-historians such as Wölfflin, for example. To these they leave the examination of what is "professional and technical." In this respect, one analyst has made the remark, "in short, our science has clarified everything concerning art but art itself." [37]

What Freud considers "the content" of art-works, into which his psychology can give us insight, is what he finds has roots or springs in unconsciousness. Consequently, what he considers the "meaning" of art-works is the descriptive significance he can give it in terms of his theory of individual psychological processes, namely: compensations for renunciations of direct instinct-gratification. This is simple enough to establish, given the over-all principle that *every* psychic phenomenon which operates in the service of "culture" is a substitute for physical phenomena in the service of "nature." It is not so much a case of Freud's considering *all* of the means by which works of art have the affective powers they do have, as it is an instance of his abstracting those elements in art-works which can be considered consistent with his psychology. Had he been interested in a more complete picture, he would have had to concern himself with the formative process itself, and with the sensuous nature of the creation which is what "moves" or "pleases" the audience most immediately rather than what gives the art-work its (Freudian) "meaning." In this connection, Marcuse, who is a sympathetic interpreter of Freud, characterizes his approach in the following way: ". . . [Freud's] 'appreciation' and enjoyment of art was somewhat limited. . . . For him . . . the enjoyment of art was possible only after he understood why he had been moved by it."[38] Given the limitations of his bio-psychological principles, Freud arbitrarily restricts the "meaning" in works of art to nothing but such "content" as can be formulated as sublimational and substitutional. Consequently, such "content" cannot have any other than retrospective significance. The best that art can offer under these circumstances is "pleasure" of an illusory nature, in contrast to the harder pleasure of reality, such as science alone offers him.

But for Jung, since it is *not* the case that *all* psychic phenomena is in the service of nature, not all the content of which has the character of substitute-gratifications, therefore: the "meaning" of all art-works is not necessarily of a retrospective significance, from the point of view of the artist, nor of illusory pleasure, from the point of view of the audience. Some of it may be; but not all. Granted that Jung, also, has not taken sufficient interest in the sensuous nature of the aesthetic creation, of the actual formative process, or the formal elements of the art-work (a lack for which even so sympathetic an interpreter as Sir Herbert Read has taken him to task),[39] the fact remains that this is a lack he shares equally with Freud.

In sum: Freud and Jung are equally "guilty" (in the eyes of more philosophical aestheticians) in being entirely too simplified in their theorctical treatment of art-works. Their "insufficiencies" express themselves in underestimations and oversimplications of both the formal and the historical elements in works of art. It must be recognized that both of them make a distinction between the *content* and the *form* of an art-work which no practicing critic could use for any but the crudest work of art (for example, to distinguish the thought from the prosody of a greeting card verse). One must simply face the fact that, exactly like Freud, and in spite of his sense of broader implications, Jung is primarily interested in what he can abstract from a work of art and interpret in terms of his theory of the unconscious. This is precisely what he means by its "psychic significance"; but this can readily be seen to be something more modest and, at the same time, more precise than Freud's conception of the "meaning" of a work of art.

These remarks concerning the limitations of both Freud's and Jung's approaches, and the principles on the basis of which Freudians distinguish the "subject matter" of art, the "meaning" of which they offer a technique for interpreting, allows us to return to the main topic of examining Jung's writings in this connection.

If there seems to be, from the side of Freud, an overlapping in theory concerning the possibility of inherited collective psychic factors of ideational content (which has not been integrated into the general structure of Freudian psychology), so is there, from the side of Jung, an overlapping in theory concerning the possibility of the "contents" of art-works being interpreted reductively, as subject matters with no more than retrospective significance (which has not been integrated into his remarks concerning art).

I am referring, of course, to the interpretation of such art-works as have been described earlier as constituting the Psychological Mode. Jung leaves his analysis of such works of art incomplete. He implies, on the one hand, that by virtue of the *subject matter* in such works having references to "all of" what goes "to make up the conscious life of man, and his feeling life in particular,"[40] and since their *methods* of representation and organization "nowhere transcend the bounds of phychological intelligibility," therefore, "there is nothing that the psychologist can add to it that the poet has not already said

in better words." In effect, the "meaning" of such art-
works is self-evident. On the other hand, he states that
there are such works of art as receive "tributaries, dark
and turbid though they be" from what he has termed the
"personal unconscious"[41] and in such cases, "if *they* become a major factor they make the work of art a symptomatic rather than symbolic product. This kind of art
might conceivably be left without injury or regret to
the Freudian purgative method."[42]

Now, it would seem that Jung has oversimplified his
schema for the modes of art and their interpretation. In
practice, he distinguishes the Psychological Mode which
requires no psychologist's explanation, and the Visionary
Mode which requires explanation on the basis of a theory
of symbolism. The former seems to be—at its best—nothing more or less than the product of consciousness; but
this he qualifies by saying that even if the artist himself
thinks of his creative process that way, the fact is that
the autonomous creative complex is not within his conscious control. At its best its meaning is self-evident; it
means what it says. The latter seems to be—at its best
or at its worst—nothing more nor less than the product
of the Collective Unconscious; but this he qualifies by
saying that even if the artist thinks of his subject matter
that way, the fact is that the formative process has been
conditioned by his conscious technical education.

Between the two modes and the ways in which he has
qualified them, it would appear that Jung has included
all of the necessary factors for understanding the relations between the conscious and unconscious elements
participating in them. But, actually, he has employed

169

principles of explanation limited to (1) consciousness and (2) the Collective Unconscious. His reference to the (3) Personal Unconscious appears only in the context of interpreting such art-works as "pretend" to be symbolical but are found to be symptomatic; and they may be left to the Freudian "purgative" method.

But what about works in the Psychological Mode at its worst, rather than at its best? Works which take their ostensible subject matter from man's conscious life and employ methods which are not strange, shocking, or unintelligible, but are, nevertheless, not "self-evident." It seems to me that Jung ignores the problem by characterizing the Psychological Mode as offering no interest to the psychologist because the subject matter and method "nowhere transcend the bounds of psychological intelligibility." What kind of psychological intelligibility would that be? Is he not tacitly implying that the Freudian detective work in search of individual unconscious "meaning" is applicable to both modes in cases where the art-work is not at the best in the mode but at its worst? That is to say, where an art-work "appears" to be in the Visionary Mode or in the Psychological Mode — in virtue of its subject matter and method—but is not successfully either (by the test that the former does not yield "a harmonious vision of fulfilment," nor the latter stimulate us to an intuition),[43] then reduction in terms of the individual psychology of the artist is useful. In effect, Freud's method can explain why a work of art in either mode is *not* successful because failure would have been caused by symptomatic features having become predominant.

I believe that the reasons for Jung's neglect of this possibility is not only his concern with distinguishing his position from that of Freud's (and not choosing to make more use of Freud's methods than he thinks he cannot avoid) but, more important, because Jung is trying to keep his focus on the work of art *from the point of view of the audience.* Therefore, he argues that, since not all psychic phenomena are to be interpreted semiotically in the service of nature, and thus understood retrospectively, his major concern is with the public and prospective meaning of Visionary art, understood symbolically. Nevertheless, it is not sufficient to state that art-works in the Psychological Mode are psychologically intelligible, unless, by implication, Jung intends for us to understand that they offer meaning of a public or social retrospective character, in contrast to works in the Visionary Mode which offer meanings of a public or social prospective character. If this is not the case, then why are art-works in the Psychological Mode self-evident? For them to mean what they say, it must be assumed that we already understand such sayings and, therefore, they must have meanings previously established in a conscious system of causal-reductive thought; they represent our conscious understanding of the past.

Consider how this might be compared with literary analyses. Jung's Psychological and Visionary Modes might reasonably be compared and contrasted with descriptions of the arts in terms of the "Beautiful" and the "Sublime," more closely, with conceptions of the "Apollonian" and "Dionysian," and the "Classical" and "Romantic."

Irving Babbitt's presentation of "Classicism" is derived from Aristotelian thought, and pursued through seventeenth and eighteenth-century French neo-classicism. His conception is that Classicism rests on the insight into a general human nature, "a core of normal experience" which all classicists affirm. "From this central affirmation derives the doctrine of imitation, and from imitation in turn the doctrines of probability and decorum."[44] In French neo-classical thought, artistic "imitation" does not rest on "immediate perception like that of the Greeks but on outer authority."[45] The result of this position is that the doctrine of imitating the externals of authoritative models is "incompatible . . . with the spontaneity of the imagination."[46]

Jacques Barzun presents an interpretation of "Romanticism" in opposition to this condition, as the champion of the imagination. He represents the movement as the opposition of individual nature to a *mistaken* conception of "general human nature"; and in its use of the spontaneous, the improbable, and the indecorous, as affirming the role of feeling, which has been under-valued in the classicist's psychology. Dean Barzun sees this as anything but an escapist's "illusion" and justifies the highly differentiated manifestations of Romanticism as expressive of the search for fact—the facts that would yield a truer conception of human life and of reality than Classicism had offered.

> Accordingly [the Romanticists] recorded the grotesque and the mystical, side by side with the trivial and the sublime. This makes their revelations

172

of the world through art a multiverse rather than a universe.[47]

By the same token, the conceptions of life and reality abstractable from their art-works are pluralistic rather than systems derivable from principles of a single character, be they psysical, biological or otherwise. The "world" which such works of art "reveals" is neither simply "objective" nor simply "subjective." It has, rather, the character that Jung would describe as "inner worldly" but not "individual"; it has the character of the Collective Unconscious.

If one maintains an analogy between Jung's Psychological Mode and "Classical" art, and his Visionary Mode with "Romantic" art, it is possible to see the "psychic significance" of these different kinds of art in the implications that certain literary critics have drawn.

In his essay "The Meaning of a Literary Idea," Lionel Trilling describes the *form* of a literary art-work as "itself an idea which controlled and brought to a particular issue the subordinate ideas it contained."[48] The "particular issue" is recognized in the effect of the art-work on the audience. Trilling is saying that a literary idea causes the "subject matter" of the work of art—rational and emotional elements—to be arranged in such an order as to lead the mind of the audience to a particular effect. The effect may be one of "fulfilment" or of "stimulation." It is possible to distinguish such effects by the pragmatic test of whether the art-work confirms the audience in its previously held beliefs (concerning human

173

life and the world) or whether it stimulates the audience to new conceptions.

Surely this latter effect is the sort of thing D. H. Lawrence had in mind when he wrote:

> The essential function of art is moral. Not aesthetic, not decorative, not pastime and recreation. But moral ... a passionate, implicit morality, not didactic. A morality which changes the blood, rather than the mind. Changes the blood first. The mind follows later....[49]

In other words, "the essential function" is that of a prospective character which brings about change by way of the unconscious ("the blood").

These various suggestions may now be correlated in the following way. "Classical" art, by dealing with the already recognized subject matter of human experience, and by virtue of the already understood meanings of its idea-forms, has as its "psychic function" — confirming the audience in its previously held beliefs and attitudes. It is in this sense that it means no more than it says. "Romantic" art, on the other hand, by dealing with previously uninterpreted subject matter, and by virtue of the "strangeness" of its idea-forms, has as its "psychic function" — stimulation of the audience to new understanding, i.e., an intuition of something not yet comprehended. It is for this reason that works of art in the Classical-Psychological-mode "appeal more vividly to our aesthetic sensibility" and "offer us an harmonious vision of fulfilment,"[50] whereas, Romantic Visionary-mode works of art are "more stimulating, drive, as it were, more deeply into

us, and therefore seldom permit us a purely aesthetic enjoyment."[51] Representative art is retrospective in its nature; symbolic art is prospective. The former yields repose
in reaffirming previously established knowledge; the latter forces the distress of giving birth to new possible-
knowledge.

These comparisons are based on analogies in the systems
of interpretation, they are not meant to pretend that such
conceptions as Barzun's ideas of Romantic art and Jung's
theory of symbolic art, for example, are identical. Special
problems exist in respect to the possibility of there being
works of Romantic art in the psychological mode as well
as in the visionary; just as there might be works of Classical art in either mode. But these subtleties would take us
too far afield·from the main line of concern.

The question should be raised whether Jung offers
nothing more to aesthetics than literary critics or cultural
historians can contribute in virtue of their descriptive
classifications. This would bring us to the heart of the
matter.

For Jung, literary and pictorial typologies such as
"Classical" and "Romantic" are primarily concerned with
distinctions laid down in respect to *style*. Both Freud and
Jung speak of the possible contribution of psychology to
aesthetics in respect to *subject matter*, having in mind such
"material" as exists outside of the work of art and to
which it "refers." They leave questions of style to what
they both imply is the sphere of "formal aesthetics." But
the difference between them seems to me perfectly clear.

The effect of the Freudian approach is that the interpretation of art would consist of (1) formal aesthetics, and (2) psychoanalytic interpretations of art-works, producing retrospective "meaning," and these together would exhaust the field of art criticism. What implications formal aesthetics might draw for the nature and meaning of art-in-general would be discounted by the Freudians as unacceptable unless it were grounded in Freudian psychology. What judgments critics of any of the arts might make would be discounted for the same reason, were they sociologically, historically, philosophically and/or economically oriented. They would not be able to interpret and explain the "meaning" of art-works.

By contrast, the effect of Jung's approach is precisely to "underwrite" just such criticism. He offers a psychological justification for all efforts at "taking art seriously." That is to say, while "formal aesthetics" seems to remain something independent—unexamined by psychoanalysis —all the various facets of art *criticism* are supported insofar as they are attempts to formulate that "previously unknown" into which the work of art gives us an intuition. Either such efforts achieve the goal of interpreting the art-work effectively, so that it functions as a reconciling (transcending) symbol, or they go beyond that to exhaust the implicit or potential reference, in which case the image that has been completely explained ceases to possess the power of a symbol and becomes a sign. But the possibilities for valuable criticism by others than psychoanalysts remain limitless.

If I read Jung correctly, then, the implication of his position is that: *critical interpretations of works of art are to a culture what the analyst's interpretations of pri-*

vate symbolic contents are to the individual patient in therapy.

There is no intention whatsoever inherent in Jung's writing on the subject which would support the idea that the analyst should supplant the critic and treat works of art as if they were patients undergoing analysis. On the contrary, his writing clearly indicates the analogy between what the patient and analyst do in trying to "read the symbol rightly" for the individual with what the audience and the critics do in trying to appreciate a work of art. The problem is to grasp as consciously as possible the prospective significance of something that is ostensibly unintelligible but "driven deeply" into consciousness and which "stimulates."

The Freudian position seems to be that critics deal only with the "surface" of a work of art and cannot (because they do not have the necessary principles and method for interpretation) understand its psychological essence—its "meaning." This is like saying: if the art-work is compared with a dream, critics are restricted to trying to draw significance from the "manifest content" without awareness that there is the more important "latent content."

But Jung's position is that, even if one were to compare the work of art with a dream—only some dreams are signs to be understood retrospectively, by a reductive method; but there are, also, dreams that are symbols and these are to be taken as giving "lines" for future development, interpreted by the "synthetic" method appropriate to *them*. The consequence of such a point of view is that, from certain works of art we can derive further understanding, new knowledge, intellectually conceivable

177

formulations of what had been intimated. The role of the critic is to make explicit, as well as he can, what is implicit in the art-work. And Jung considers this an entirely legitimate, valuable, intellectual function—independent of psychology.

In effect, Jung's writings on art present a defense of criticism. Analytic psychology is not the only means of interpreting art-works. It is no substitute for criticism, for formal aesthetics, or for philosophies of art. Its sole function is *to give a psychological justification for efforts to interpret works of art* as an enterprise worthy of respect in its own right. If the theory of psychology which Jung has elaborated—including ideas of the archetypes of the Collective Unconscious—is directly of use to art critics, so much the better. But his general theory is no substitute for actual criticism, any more than it is a substitute for a patient's psychoanalysis. Nor does he claim for it the importance which followers of Freud have made for reductive art criticism. In his two, relatively short, essays on the arts, Jung himself has produced practically none of the possible consequences that might be derived from a careful and detailed application of his principles and method to particular works of art. (Actually, a number of critics have begun trying to do this, with varying degrees of success. There are such examples as Theodora Ward's study of Emily Dickinson, Sir Herbert Read's criticism of painting in *Education through Art*, James Baird's study of *Moby Dick*, Wingfield Digby's *Symbol and Image in William Blake*, Erich Neumann's analysis of the "Cupid and Psyche" of Apuleius, Walter Abell's *The Collective Dream in Art*, and Maud Bodkin's *Studies of*

Type-Images.[52] On the other hand, in his numerous and extensive books, Jung has attempted to make a substantial contribution to the theory of symbolism that would assure the validity of the critical enterprise in general, within which the above cited examples can be included; they would not constitute the exclusive body of what "qualifies" as criticism.

When an anti-Jungian like Edward Glover is confronted with this position, he interprets Jung to mean that "If . . . the psychologist could be relied on to uncover the casual connections within a work of art and in the process of artistic creation, he would leave the study of art no ground to stand on and would reduce it to a special branch of his own science."[53] Glover, thereupon, makes the judgment that Jung offers only a "frivolous excuse for ignorance."[54] Obviously, he misses the whole point. It is not "ignorance" which Jung is defending; he is concerned with delimiting the sphere proper to psychology in relation to the arts (a defense of criticism) from the mixed mode of criticism-and-psychologizing which the Freudian recommends. It is criticism that is useful in cultural, public, appreciation of the art-work as a finished, independent, product. The Freudian criticism-and-psychologizing is useful only in respect to the art-work as a fuction in the artist's psychology—where it is not taken "seriously," but used as an instrument for analysis.

When a literary critic such as William York Tindall, writing specifically about symbolic literature, speaks of the art-work as suggesting "more thoughts and feelings than we could state," so that "if we stated as many as we could . . . some would be left over and some would remain unstatable,"[55] he is both implicitly supporting Jung's thesis, and explicitly affirming the function of criticism, namely, to abstract and conceptualize, as well as possible, the thought and feeling content of the art-work. This does not explain "away" the art-work by uncovering casual connections or the creative process; rather, it draws the implications of "meaning" (psychic significance) by establishing warrantable relations between what is present in the work and something else, whether the latter comes from sociological, historical, mythological, or political thought, etc. Such specific criticisms are bound to overlap. But this is an advantage, not a drawback. It has the advantage of increasing and extending conscious understanding (new knowledge) which could be met with opposition only by such an "aesthetics" as sees just one form of criticism as exclusively exhaustive of "meaning."

Whether Lionel Trilling writes criticism of Jane Austen (whose novels seem to exemplify the Psychological mode, both in subject matter and method) whether Wallace Fowlie writes criticism of Arthur Rimbaud (whose poetry seems to exemplify the Visionary Mode, both in subject matter and method), or whether Erich Auerbach writes of Virginia Woolf (whose novels seem a complex of method and subject matter in both modes) —the nature of criticism is approximately the same: to abstract and conceptualize the thought and feeling content implicit in the work, and to elicit its meaning in relation with other relevant values. It is precisely this function which Jung's reflections on art serve as a means of defense; it "protects" it by offering, in a conceptual framework, a psychological justification for its validity.

To be sure, in making his defense, Jung appears to have been interested in symbolic art to the exclusion of art in the Psychological Mode. But I think this is only a consequence of his having "bent over backwards" to support as useful for society just that kind of art which Freudian analysis implies is most idiosyncratic, and therefore of "meaning" only in the psychology of the individual artist. Consequently, given Jung's distinction between signs and symbols, it may be seen that *works in the Psychological Mode function as signs; works in the Visionary Mode function as symbols*. Obviously, the acid test is whether the "signal" art-work does *reaffirm* one's previously established knowledge and values, and whether the "symbolic" art-work does *stimulate* one to new knowledge and new values.

New knowledge of what? It is clear that works of art are not propositions of a scientific nature. Their "statements" are not to be taken as referring to "matters of fact," or "a state of affairs" in any physical scientific sense. Such "statements" may be included as constituents within a verbal or iconographic unit, but the work-as-a-whole is not reducible to them. They are, as Lionel Trilling has put it, among the "elements"—rational, moral, or emotional—that are organized and controlled by the form. Therefore, the effect of the whole (controlled by an "idea-form") is the subject matter of the critic's interpretation. Now, this will be true of both cases. In Psychological ("signal") Mode art-works as well as in Visionary ("symbolic") Mode works, it is the idea-form of the whole from which the critic is making his abstractions and to which he is bringing his relevant comparative data. In both cases, the effect of the whole art-work is on the whole psychic reality of the audience. What else can be meant by the work of art making possible communication from "the spirit and heart of the *poet as man* to the spirit and heart of mankind," as Jung puts it?

The organization that this "whole" determines is conventionally divided, by critics, between "thought and feeling." The new knowledge, critically derivable from the art-work, therefore, is usually spoken of as a re-organization of thought or of feeling. But Jung points out that there is more to consciousness than that, and there is more to psychic life than just consciousness. Among conscious functions must be included, besides thinking and feeling, also, sensing and intuiting. The former two are more amenable to criticism because they are both "rational" functions, i.e., they give conceptual meaning and understanding by means of causal relations (thinking) and make value judgments (feeling). The latter two are less amenable to criticism because they are both "irrational" functions, i.e., the content of perception (sensing) and insights into future possibilities (intuition). Beyond consciousness must be included both the Personal and the Collective Unconscious.

The result of this psychological differentiation is that Jung must say: the organization that the idea-form gives to the "whole" of the work of art has its effect on the whole psychic life of the audience. The effect, then, is a re-organization of psychic life, in general, not just an appeal to "thought" or "feeling." In any case, it is always true that the work of art must appeal first to sensing, and this in itself is not adequately understood. But, besides that, it would seem to follow that criticism has limited itself unfairly by concentrating on thought and feeling.

Granted that these are the two conscious functions to which works of art in the Psychological Mode do appeal, it is a Procrustes' bed on which to mutilate symbolic values if critics limit themselves to interpreting art-works in the Visionary Mode by the same standards. In effect, Jung is offering the critics a justification for a truer, fuller, more accurate and adequate interpretation of symbolic works by establishing a psychological theory in which *intuition* has an understandable role to play, or purpose to fulfil.

It is comparable to the role that individual symbols play in a patient's therapy, that is, a compensatory function between archetypes of the Collective Unconscious and a present state of consciousness, and a prospective significance, intuitive of a line for future development. For culture, just as for therapy, symbols are not intuitions by themselves; they are only the brute facts that must be interpreted. Herein lies the inestimable importance of the critical enterprise. Without the "right" conscious interpretation, the symbol remains only an uncomprehended "event." With the "right" interpretation it can become a "living experience"—contributing to the betterment of the patient, in one case, and of the society, in the other.

Whether or not an interpretation is "right" is decided pragmatically, i.e., by whether it does *work* to bring about an advance. The "betterment" in both cases rests on the reconciling power of the symbol, a potentiality that can become effective in practice only by way of conscious appreciation. In the case of culture, it is critical intelligence, the activity of criticism that performs this function.

At the very least, then, such "new knowledge" as is derived from a symbol, by the critical appreciation, is of value to the progressive re-organization of psychic life as a whole. It cannot qualify as knowledge in the sense that logical empiricism limits "knowledge" to the mathematical and physical sciences. It would appear to be closer to such "knowledge" as we call "wisdom." Wisdom literature is conventionally thought of as concerned with making connections between "knowledge" and "life." And, in this respect, it would be easy to see that the popularity and importance of literary criticism, in particular, exemplifies the common public desire for contemporary wisdom literature. By drawing out relationships between certain art-works and other relevant values, such criticism offers interpretations of art-works that "stimulate" but are not self-evident. The new knowledge (the "wisdom") of such criticism lies in its appreciation of the intuitive or prospective values of the art-works; and its effectiveness lies in its ability to make connections between the symbol and a re-organization of psychic life. If the interpretation is "right" it does bring about an improvement in the service of "wholeness." If it is not "right," and the advance is not derived from it, then the "symbol" remains only an uncomprehended "event." The valuable critic, like the effective analyst, is the one who helps the audience (like the cooperating patient) to interpret those manifestations that are symbolic in purport.

SECTION 3: *Symbolism and Epistemology*

By so doing, he exemplifies the expression of "wisdom," relating what is known to proposals for how to live better.

This is not the only function of criticism, just as the interpretation of genuine symbols is not the only function of therapy. But by concentrating his defense of artworks on this special interest, Jung has offered a *psychological* justification for the critical enterprise in general.

SECTION 3: *Symbolism and Epistemology*

Ira Progoff has pointed out that there was a strong influence of Kantian thought on the formulation of Jung's primary principles. "He accepted Kant's fundamental restriction that we cannot know things in themselves, and he concluded that the only reality we can study with confidence is *Esse in Anima,* Being in the Soul." Subsequently developing his interpretation of what is "psychologically real," Jung maintains that "the phenomena of the psyche constitute an area of reality which may be studied in their own terms."

> In interpreting Jung's point of view, we must always remember the fact that all his doctrines about the "world" as cosmos are based, not on the world itself, but on the analysis of psychic content.[56]

What is loosely called "the world itself," then, may be generally thought of as "physical reality" in contradistinction to "psychic reality." The problems of knowledge concerning "physical reality" may be conceived as essentially theoretical, and studied by methods appropriate to it. But the problems of knowledge concerning "psychic reality" must be recognized to be essentially practical and, therefore, "studied in their own terms." The "terms" of "psychic reality" are conditioned by the manifestations of psychic life in unconscious as well as in conscious activity. This is the radical originality of Freud's interpretation of psychology.

Jung believes he has made an important improvement over the Freudian system by introducing an equally radical distinction within the area of unconscious manifestations. Such phenomena *are* what they *do* for us. What they do is governed by laws inherent in the psyche, some of which can be known and expressed in the language of instincts and their transformations. Manifestations of these will be *signs*. What they do for us is offer "hints" as to why we are as we are; and by a casual-reductive analysis, with the help of such "clues," the analyst can discover the aetiology of the condition they represent.

But the practical concern for psychotherapy is that of curing the patient and, even when all such aetiological analysis has been made, the most important question remains: how should the patient *develop* healthily? Unless this is imposed from some public system of behavior independent of the individual patient, the source of such "knowledge" must be, somehow, within him. In other words, even after the reductive analysis of the *signs* has revealed the causes and, it is hoped, removed the power of such causes, so that the patient is "free" where he had previously been "possessed," the problem remains of what he *should* "freely" make of himself.

Jung's conception is that there are such psychic manifestations as must be designated *symbols* which, arising from the unconscious, offer "hints" or "clues" of what one ought to become. These are necessarily individual, and must *not* be retrospectively analysed, but interpreted appropriately to the individual's prospective development. Such phenomena as these, likewise, are governed by laws inherent in the psyche, but they are not clearly known. They are not to be described in terms of instincts and their transformations. They appear as "images" and, being recognized in a variety of universal manifestations, are characterized as archetypes of a Collective Unconscious. The "terms," then, of their description will be metaphoric and their vocabulary mythological.

By interpretation of them what is gained is "knowledge" of the individual, for the individual. This is *personal knowledge* of the psychic reality of the individual, oriented toward the future and conceived as contributing to that individual's psychic health (expressed metaphorically as "wholeness"). Either such an intuition is proved "right" because the development undertaken on the basis of the interpretation does conduce to "wholeness" or it is proved "wrong" when that does not happen. The interpretation is always problematic, but supported by the fact that Jung finds much evidence of there being successfully interpreted intuitions.

It is necessary to recognize that Jung considers the symbol to be a spontaneous formation, the content of which is from the Collective Unconscious. It is able to function in consciousness only when it has been "channelized" by interpretation. "If the symbol is joined with the ego so that it becomes the center of consciousness, and if it is experienced inwardly with an intimate sense of personal identification, it becomes the focus for the major energies of the individual."[57] Without the operation of critical consciousness, it is unlikely that the symbol can have this effect; in its place, then, the public symbols of the individual's culture serve as "impersonal" substitutes. The result is that the individual never achieves *personal knowledge* and never achieves the "wholeness" which is authentic to himself.

Among the "impersonal" substitutes are the symbols of religion and art. The most striking difference between the two, of course, is that "art" never functions in an official or systematic way.

Theoretical knowledge may be intellectually possessed without making any appreciable difference whatsoever to the individual's inner life. But "knowledge" of one's own psychic reality is meaningless except as practical knowledge — such interpretations as contribute to changing how one lives. Analogously, the kind of "knowledge" derived from interpretations of works of art is practical knowledge; it re-organizes the psychic reality as a whole. The essential elements of this reality are consciousness, the personal and the collective unconscious. Works of art in the Psychological Mode, it would seem, act as mediators between consciousness and the personal unconscious. Works of art in the Visionary Mode act as mediators between consciousness and the Collective Unconscious. Since these symbols are public or "impersonal" (suprapersonal) they are not, comparatively, as powerfully effective as individual symbols. But their "psychic significance" is that they demand interpretation from the person who is "seized" by them; and, insofar as an individual takes from his interpretation of them some insight of a prospective nature for himself, the symbolic work of art is of comparable value. In this sense, art is the public dream of a society. Relative to the degree of integration of a society, its art will be expressive of the archetypes of the Collective Unconscious working out compensatory "indicators" of how it should tend to develop. That is, it presents an intuition of what is "missing."

There is a lack in Jung's presentation of his ideas concerning the creative process in art, despite the fact that he sees it as analogous with the process of symbol formation in individual psychology. This is because a "vision," as experienced by a patient in analysis, exists apart from its expression, whereas no "work" of art can. As to the "spontaneous formation," Jung explains it as a result of an autonomous complex in the artist as in the patient. But he never makes an adequate statement of what constitutes the *creative* autonomous complex. This is clearly related to the fact that he does not pay any close attention to the so-called "formative process." As a result, he does not specify the differentia by which the creative autonomous complex in the arts can be distinguished from the autonomous complex operating in other spheres of creativity—"the seer, prophet, leader and enlightener."

This also reminds the reader of a certain imprecision and, consequent, ambiguity in Jung's expressions concerning "form" and "matter" in a work of art. Sometimes the content of a symbol is spoken of as the "matter" which the Collective Unconscious produces spontane-

189

ously (of an archetypal nature). When this is true of a work of art, the artist is said to "form" (shape) the matter. On the other hand, some of the time Jung speaks of the archetype as a "form" (in the sense of a blueprint) which the artist then "shapes" his "material" (his medium?) in order to objectify. The ambiguity, perhaps, arises not so much from the metaphoric language which Jung employs as from the comparisions of statements made at different times and in different contexts, while within any one such context of thought Jung uses the words consistently. This is why I have preferred to speak of "subject matter" and "method," when dealing with these questions.

Despite this lack and this ambiguity, it must be recognized that from the very beginning of this inquiry it has been obvious that Jung is interested in symbolism as a heuristic device. "The effective symbol" is a guide to discovery. The genuine symbol, both private and public, is conceived as enabling the individual and the society to fulfil an educative requirement. It is true that this is not the theoretical knowledge of the physical sciences which he has in mind, but the "practical knowledge" of "psychic reality." He is not interested in what is fruitless for psychic life, but what is "pregnant with meaning." Only the "event" that may be interpreted successfully attracts him; not the would-be symbol, a "manufactured" item that is impotent. And success is discoverable through effectiveness in what actually develops in the future.

This aspect of futurity, the concern with what is tending to become, the intuitive perception, with prospective value, leading to further discovery in enacted life, valued more highly because of its consequent contribution to "wholeness"—all of these aspects of the symbol bespeak its function as a heuristic device in the service of practical personal knowledge. The most distinguishing feature of all of this is the concern with "the possible" as contrasted with "the actual." Reductive analysis of *signs* operates in the service of discovering the conditioning causes of "the actual." Synthetic interpretation of *symbols* operates in the service of discovering what the indications from the Collective Unconscious are for the future. It is in this respect that they are seen to be concerned with what is the most appropriate "possible" for an individual. From Jung's point of view, it is patently arbitrary to speak of any other source of information as to what any particular person ought to become.

Such indications—adumbrations, intimations, intuitions—of "the possible" can be formulated as *personal knowledge* only through the activity of interpretation; and validated only through the pragmatic test. This is the structure of an epistemological analysis of Jung's conception of symbolism. His greatest concern is with the usefulness of such means for the on-going understanding of "psychic reality." But, by extrapolation, he indicates that such an epistemological analysis might, also be made of the rational sciences of "physical reality." Between the world of private "psychic reality" and the public world of scientific "physical reality," stand the public symbolic systems of religion and art. Halfway between—in virtue of the fact that, while they take their "subject matter" from the realm of what is psychologically real, they use such "methods" as are appropriate to an interpersonal rather than an individual application.

When writing on a general theory of individual psychology, Jung distinguishes such psychic manifestations as *signs*, in the sirvice of *Life*, from *symbols*, in the service of *Spirit*. When he speaks of public symbolic systems, *Life* is equated with "Nature," *Spirit* with "Culture"; and "Culture" is no substitute for the gratifications of "Nature." The difference between his system of thought and Freud's is that Jung requires more than one kind of principle for explanation.

It is curious that Freud considers his psychology "dualistic" and that of Jung "monistic." Freud writes:

> Our views have from the very first been *dualistic*, and to-day they are even more definitely dualistic than before—now that we describe the opposition as being, not between ego instincts and sexual instincts but between life instincts and death instincts. Jung's libido theory is on the contrary *monistic*; the fact that he calls his one instinctual force "libido" is bound to cause confusion, but need not affect us otherwise.[58]

The confusion arises, obviously, over the fact that for Freud two kinds of instincts (life and death), neither of which is reducible to the other, constitute a dualism of principles for explanation. Whereas, from Jung's point of view, since both life and death instincts are *instincts*, Freud's system is "monistic." It is Jung's theory that is genuinely a dualism. Psychic energy in the service of "life" cannot be reduced to psychic energy in service of "spirit," nor vice versa. But only the libido of "life" energy is *instinctual*. The psychic energy of all manifestations of the unconscious in the service of "spirit" is *symbolical*. Exactly what it has its source *in* is not known. Jung never defines the "objective reality" of the archetypes of the Collective Unconscious; he makes no statements whatsoever concerning their "ontological nature." It is only a misinterpreter like Glover who believes that Jung has so defined them—perhaps in the sense of an "Objective Spirit" such as one finds in 19th century German Idealism—who, therefore, accuses Jung of "animism."[59]

Jung speaks of the archetypes only as a "subjective reality"—they are psychologically real. But since they are of a radically different nature than *instincts*, which have their sources in biological reality, it is his system, in contrast with Freud's that is "dualistic." Instincts and Archetypes are truly two different, opposed, principles for the interpretation of individual psychology; whereas "life instincts" and "death instincts" are both of the same causal nature.

In a sense, Freud had conceived the opposition in psychology to be ultimately rooted in the conflict between what is biological and what is inorganic. For Jung, this would be explained by the fact that Freud had not taken seriously all of the special characteristics of what is "psychologically real." The cause of this would be Freud's desire to approximate the methods of scientifically analysing the "physically real" in constructing his conceptual analysis of "psychic reality." Since the archetypes cannot be reduced to biological instincts, therefore, Freud's own reflections on phylogenetic traces in psychic

193

heredity remained unintegrated with his general system. What is at stake, on the one hand, is (a) the nature of "knowledge" in psychology; on the other hand, it is (b) an adequate conception of "psychic reality."

(a) If it is stipulated that only what satisfies the logical empiricists' criteria of "scientific language" can qualify as "knowledge," then Freud's system is, at least, *closer* to being knowledge than Jung's is. But this is because Freud was, himself, trying to maintain the kind of standards that the (subsequent) development of positivistic thought has sharpened and codified. On the other hand, Jung appeals to the Kantian rather than the Comtian tradition in respect to epistemology. And, in so doing, his theory of symbolism, itself, offers a challenge to the philosophy of science. Such a philosopher as Cassirer may be called upon to give support to his efforts. Polanyi's recent book on *Personal Knowledge* must be considered an example of the work possible in the direction of a more accurate epistemology, taking into account the conception of personal, practical, knowledge implicit in Jung's position.

> Man lives in a symbolic universe. Language, myth, art and religion are parts of this universe. They are the varied threads which weave the symbolic net, the tangled web of human experience. . . . No longer can man confront reality immediately; he cannot see it, as it were, face to face. Physical reality seems to recede in proportion as man's symbolic activity advances. Instead of dealing with the things themselves man is in a sense constantly *conversing with himself*.

194

He has so enveloped himself in linguistic forms, in artistic images, in mythical symbols or religious rites that he cannot see or know anything except by the interposition of this artificial medium. His situation is the same in the theoretical as in the practical sphere. Even here man does not live in a world of hard facts, or according to his immediate needs and desires. He lives rather in the midst of imaginary emotions, in hopes and fears, in illusions and disillusions, in his fantasies and dreams.[60]

Cassirer's metaphoric phrase of man "conversing with himself" is an analogue for what Jung has been trying to describe all along as the "conversation" between the conscious mind and the Collective Unconscious, in which "himself" becomes the facet of psychic reality which is supra-personal. As a practising psychotherapist, for Jung, the most obvious importance of this "conversation" is that it results in the discovery of "lines" for future development. His position is perfectly clear: any psychology that does not reckon with his source of *personal knowledge* cannot offer a basis for coping with any other manifestation of "Spirit" or "Culture." And, by the same token, no epistemology that ignores the function of intuition can be adequate for all kinds of knowledge.

(b) Edward Glover interprets Jung's conception of the function of a Collective Unconscious as a "devaluation of individual factors"[61]—the empirical conditioning of the individual. And, as a result, Jung carries this "devaluation"

to its logical conclusion by denying the individual

195

man whatever credit or comfort he might derive from his artistic achievements.[62]

What the Freudian assumes is that we understand with certainty what constitutes *the individual man*. But this is precisely what differences among psychological theories point out that we do not understand with certainty. The Freudian Glover appears to be defending the individual's "credit" relative only to this victory at the conscious level in the struggle between consciousness and the (Jungian) Personal Unconscious. Were the Jungian hypothesis of a Collective Unconscious confirmed, Glover would feel that the individual's "credit" is lost, because consciousness was not the source of what? — the subject matter or the method? — out of which artistic achievements are accomplished.

It is only if we are blinded by the idea of the archetypes, so that we no longer recognize all that has been said about the role of consciousness in interpreting as well as in objectifying symbols, that we can imagine Jung means all the "credit" for such "achievements" goes to the Collective Unconscious.

But the problem is analogous in Freudian psychology itself. What is the relationship, in terms of "credit" (responsibility, praise, and blame), between the impersonal factors (the Id) and the personal ones (Ego consciousness)? Jung's distinctions would make the impersonal factors not simply opposed to the personal-conscious ones, but participating with them in order to achieve a progressive development. In both cases there is a social relativity between what is characterized as personal and impersonal. The element of struggle is described in one system as the conflict between life and death instincts; in the other as the conflict between Life and Spirit. Jung's concern with the element of futurity as a positive "interest" of the unconscious is the crucial difference to set in contrast with the exclusive concern of Freudian retrospective reductive analysis. The better psychology is the one that gives us more practical knowledge of "psychic reality."

Bibliography
Notes
Index of Proper
Names

Bibliography

Abell, Walter. *The Collective Dream in Art.* Cambridge: Harvard University Press, 1957.

————. "Toward a Unified Field in Aesthetics," in *Journal of Aesthetics and Art Criticism*, Vol. X, No. 3. Baltimore: The American Society for Aesthetics, 1952.

Auerbach, Erich. *Mimesis.* New York: A Doubleday Anchor Book, 1957.

Babbitt, Irving. *Rousseau and Romanticism.* New York: Meridian, 1955.

Baird, James, *Ishmael.* Baltimore: John Hopkins Press, 1956.

Barzun, Jacques. *Romanticism and the Modern Ego.* Boston: Little, Brown & Co., 1947.

Blanchard, B. *The Nature of Thought.* London: Allen & Unwin, 1939.

Bodkin, Maud. *Studies of Type Images in Poetry, Religion, and Philosophy.* Oxford: Oxford University Press, 1951.

Bowra, C. M. *The Heritage of Symbolism.* London: Macmillan, 1943.

Brumm, Ursula. "Symbolism and the Novel," in *Partisan Review*, Summer, 1958. New York: Foundation for Cultural Projects, 1958.

Bryson, Finkelstein, MacIver, and McKeon. *Symbols and Values.* New York: Harper & Brothers, 1954.

Campbell, Joseph (ed.) *Man and Time, Papers from the Eranos Yearbook*, Vol. 3. New York: Pantheon Books, 1957.

————(ed.). *Spirit and Nature, Papers from the Eranos Yearbooks*, Vol. 1. New York: Pantheon Books, 1954.

————(ed.). *The Mysteries, Papers from the Eranos Yearbooks*, Vol. 2. New York: Pantheon Books, 1955.

Cassirer, Ernst. *An Essay on Man.* New York: Doubleday Anchor Books, 1953.

————. *Language and Myth.* New York: Harper & Brothers, 1946.

————. *Philosophy of Symbolic Form*, Vol. 2. New Haven: Yale University Press, 1955.

Demos, R. "Jung's Thought and Influence," in *The Review of Metaphysics*, Vol. IX, No. 1. New Haven: The Review of Metaphysics, 1955.

Digby, G. F. Wingfield. *Symbol and Image in William Blake*. Oxford: Clarendon Press, 1957.

Fenichel, O. *The Psychoanalytic Theory of Neurosis*. London: Routledge & Kegan Paul, 1945.

Fiedler, Leslie. "Archetype and Signature," *Art and Psychoanalysis*. New York: Criterion Books, 1957.

Fowlie, Wallace. *Rimbaud*. New York: New Directions, 1946.

Freud, Sigmund. *Beyond the Pleasure Principle*. New York: Liveright, 1950.

————. *Civilization and Its Discontents*. London: The Hogarth Press, 1951.

————. *Collected Papers*, Vol. IV, London: Hogarth Press & the International Psychoanalytic Library, 1925.

————. *The Ego and the Id*. London: The Hogarth Press, 1947.

————. *The Future of an Illusion*. New York: Doubleday Anchor Books, 1957.

Glover, Edward. *Freud or Jung?* New York: Meridian Books, 1957.

Gruessen, J. J. *The Philosophic Implications of C. G. Jung's Individuation Process*. Washington, D. C.: Printed privately (M.A. Thesis), 1955.

Hacker, Frederick J. "On Artistic Productions," *Explorations in Psychoanalysis* (Robert Lindner, ed.) New York: Julian Press, 1953.

Hayes, Dorsha. "Heart of Darkness," in *Spring, 1956*. New York: Printed privately for the Analytical Psychology Club, 1956.

————. "Our Relationship to the Artist," in *Spring, 1954*. New York: Printed privately for the Analytical Psychology Club, 1954.

Henderson, B. "Thomas Mann's Drama of Love and Death," in *Spring, 1944*. New York: Printed privately for the Analytical Psychology Club, 1944.

Henderson, J. "On Dante," in *Spring, 1945*. New York: Printed privately for the Analytical Psychology Club, 1945.

Herskovits, Melville J. *Man and His Works*. New York: Alfred A. Knopf, 1956.

Hoppin, Hector. "The Psychology of the Artist," in *Spring, 1947*. New York: Printed Privately for the Analytical Psychology Club, 1947.

Hyman, Stanley Edgar. "Maud Bodkin and Psychological Criticism," *Art and Psychoanalysis*. New York: Criterion Books, 1957.

Jacobi, Jolande. *The Psychology of C. G. Jung.* New Haven: Yale University Press, 1954.

Jones, Ernest. *Papers on Psychoanalysis.* London: Bailliere, Tindall & Cox, 1948.

————. *Sigmund Freud, Life and Work,* Vol. II. London: The Hogarth Press, 1955.

Jung, C. G. *Contributions to Analytical Psychology.* New York: Harcourt, Brace & Co., 1928.

————. *Essays on a Science of Mythology.* New York: Pantheon Books, 1949.

————. "Joyce's *Ulysses*," in *Spring, 1949.* New York: Printed privately for the Analytical Psychology Club, 1949.

————. *Modern Man in Search of a Soul.* New York: Harcourt, Brace & Co., 1933.

————. *Psyche and Symbol* (Violet de Laszlo, ed.) New York: Doubleday Anchor Books, 1958.

————. *Psychological Types.* London: Routledge & Kegan Paul, 1953.

————. *Psychology and Alchemy.* New York: Pantheon, 1953.

————. *Psychology and Religion: West and East.* New York: Pantheon, 1958.

————. *Symbols of Transformation.* London: Routledge & Kegan Paul, 1956.

————. *The Development of Personality.* London: Routledge & Kegan Paul, 1954.

————. *The Integration of the Personality.* London: Routledge & Kegan Paul, 1952.

————and Pauli, W. *The Interpretation of Nature and the Psyche.* New York: Pantheon Books, 1955.

————. "The Spirit of Psychology," *Spirit and Nature.* New York: Pantheon Books, 1956.

————. *The Transcendent Function.* Zürich: Printed privately for the Students Association of the Jung Institute, 1957.

————. *Two Essays on Analytical Psychology.* New York: Meridian Books, 1956.

————. *Zur Psychologie und Pathologie sog. okkulter Phänomene.* Leipzig: Oswald Muntze, 1902.

Kaplan, Abraham. "Freud and Modern Philosophy," *Freud and the 20th Century.* (Benjamin Nelson, ed.) New York: Meridian, 1957.

Kardiner, Abram. *The Individual and His Society.* New York: Columbia University Press, 1939.

Kardiner, Abram, et al. *The Psychological Frontiers of Society.* New York: Columbia University Press, 1945.

Kaufmann, Walter. *Critique of Religion and Philosophy.* New York: Harper & Brothers, 1958.

Kazin, Alfred. "Psychoanalysis and Literature Today," in *Partisan Review,* Winter, 1959. New York: Foundation for Cultural Projects, 1959.

Kris, Ernst. *Psychoanalytic Explorations in Art.* New York: International Universities Press, 1952.

Langer, Susanne K. *Philosophy in a New Key.* New York: Pelican Books, 1948.

Lawrence, D. H. *Selected Essays.* London: Penguin Books, 1950.

Marcuse, Ludwig. "Freud's Aesthetics," *Journal of Aesthetics and Art Criticism,* Vol. XVII, No. 1. Baltimore: The American Society for Aesthetics, 1958.

Mills, George. "Art: An Introduction to Qualitative Anthropology," in *Journal of Aesthetics and Art Criticism,* Vol. XVI, No. 1. Baltimore: The American Society for Aesthetics, 1957.

Morris, Charles. *Foundations of the Theory of Signs.* Chicago: University of Chicago Press, 1938.

Moustakes, C. E. (ed.). *The Self: Explorations in Personal Growth.* New York: Harper & Brothers, 1956.

Neumann, Erich. *Amor and Psyche.* New York: Pantheon Books, 1956.

————. "Art and Time," in *Eranos Yearbook, 1951.* Zürich: Rhein Verlag, 1951.

Phillips, William (ed.). *Art and Psychoanalysis.* New York: Criterion Books, 1957.

Polanyi, Michael. *Personal Knowledge.* Chicago: University of Chicago Press, 1958.

Progoff, Ira. *Jung's Psychology and Its Social Meaning.* New York: Grove Press, 1953.

Read, Sir Herbert. "Dynamics of Art," in *Eranons Yearbook, 1952.* Zürich: Rhein Verlag, 1952.

————.*Education through Art.* New York: Pantheon Books, 1946.

————. "Poetic Consciousness and Creative Experience," *Eranos Yearbook, 1956.* Zürich: Rhein Verlag, 1956.

Sapir, Edward. *Selected Writings* (David G. Mandelbaum, ed.). Berkeley: University of California Press, 1951.

Spengler, Oswald. *The Decline of the West.* London: Allen & Unwin, 1922.

Tindall, William York. *The Literary Symbol.* Bloomington: Indiana University Press, 1955.

Trilling, Lionel. *The Liberal Imagination.* New York: Viking, 1950.

————. *The Opposing Self.* New York: Viking, 1955.

Ward, Theodora. "Ourself behind Ourself, An Interpretation of the

Crisis in the Life of Emily Dickinson," *Harvard Library Bulletin*, Vol. X, No. 1. Cambridge: Harvard University Press, 1956.
Wickes, Frances. "The Creative Process," in *Spring, 1948*. New York: Printed privately for the Analytical Psychology Club, 1948.
Wimsatt, William K., Jr., and Brooks, Cleanth. *Literary Criticism: A Short History*. New York: Alfred A. Knopf, 1957.

Notes

Introduction

[1]William Phillips (ed.), *Art and Psychoanalysis*, New York: Criterion Books, 1957.

[2]Ernest Jones, *Sigmund Freud, Life & Work*, Vol. II, London: The Hogarth Press, 1955, p. 9.

[3]Ernest Jones, *op. cit.*, p. 162.

[4]*Ibid.*, pp. 396/7.

[5]C. G. Jung, *The Integration of the Personality*, London: Routledge & Kegan Paul, 1952, p. 43.

PART 1

Section 1

[1]"On the Relation of Analytical Psychology to Poetic Art," in *Contributions to Analytical Psychology*, New York: Harcourt, Brace & Co., 1928, p. 231.

[2]"On Psychical Energy," *ibid.*, pp. 55/56.

[3]*Ibid.*, p. 232.

[4]*Ibid.*, pp. 52/53.

Section 2

[5]Bryson, Finkelstein, MacIver, and McKeon, *Symbols and Values*, New York: Harper, 1954, pp. 21, 73 ff., 170.

[6]Charles Morris, *Foundation of the Theory of Signs*, Chicago: University of Chicago Press, 1938, *passim*.

[7]O. Spengler, *The Decline of the West*, London: Allen & Unwin, 1922, p. 167.

[8]Ernst Cassirer, *An Essay on Man*, New York: Doubleday Anchor Books, 1953, pp. 56/57.

[9]Walter Kaufmann, *Critique of Religion and Philosophy*, New York: Harper, 1958, p. 139.

[10]Susanne K. Langer, *Philosophy in a New Key*, New York: Pelican Books, 1948, p. 51.

[11]*Ibid.*, pp. 48/49. (Italics as in original.)

Section 3

[12]*Two Essays on Analytical Psychology*, New York: Meridian Books, 1956, p. 218.

[13]*Psychological Types*, p. 295.

Section 4

[14]*Two Essays . . .*, p. 216.

[15]*Ibid.*, p. 121.

Section 5

[16]*Modern Man in Search of a Soul*, New York: Harcourt, Brace & Co., 1933, pp. 134/5.

[17]Jolande Jacobi, *The Psychology of C. G. Jung*, New Haven: Yale University Press, 1954, p. 39.

[18]*Two Essays . . .*, p. 277.

[19]*Modern Man . . .*, p. 138.

[20]*Two Essays . . .*, p. 278.

[21]*Ibid.*, pp. 282/3.

[22]*Psychological Types*, p. 616.

[23]"The Spirit of Psychology" in *Spirit and Nature*, New York: Pantheon Books, 1956, p. 436. (Italics mine.)

[24]*Symbols of Transformation*, London: Routledge & Kegan Paul, 1956, p. 157.

[25]*Two Essays*, p. 108.

[26]*Symbols of Transformation*, p. 368.

[27]*Psychological Types*, p. 467.

[28]*Psychological Types*, p. 556.

[29]*Contributions . . .*, p. 246.

[30]*The Integration of the Personality*, p. 53.

[31]C. G. Jung, *Essays on a Science of Mythology*, New York: Pantheon, 1949, p. 104.

[32]*Psychological Types*, p. 560.

Section 6

[33]*Ibid.*, p. 601.

[34]*The Integration of the Personality*, p. 57.

[35]*Two Essays . . .*, p. 299.

[36]*Essays on a Science . . .*, p. 109.

[37]*Two Essays . . .*, p. 299.

[38]*Ibid.*, p. 606. (Italics mine.)

[39]*Psychological Types*, pp. 609/10.

[40]*Two Essays . . .*, p. 77.

[41]*Ibid.*, p. 78 (Italics mine.)

[42]*Psychological Types*, p. 603.

[43]*Ibid.*, p. 275.

[44]*Ibid.*, p. 277.

[45]*Ibid.*, pp. 596/7.

[46]*Ibid.*, p. 272.

PART II

Section 1

[1]C. G. Jung, *Modern Men in Search of a Soul*, New York: Harcourt, Brace & Co., 1933, p. 196.

[2]*Ibid.*, p. 193.

[3]*Ibid.*, p. 194. (Italics mine.)

[4]C. G. Jung, *Contributions to Analytical Psychology*, London; Routledge & Kegan Paul Ltd., 1928, pp. 226/7.

[5]*Ibid.*, p. 231.

[6]*Ibid.*, p. 232. (Italics mine.)

[7]*Ibid.*, pp. 242/3.

[8]Reprinted in English in *Contributions to Analytical Psychology*. See note 4, this chapter.

[9]Reprinted in English in *Modern Man in Search of a Soul*. See note 1, this chapter.

Section 2

[10]*Modern Man in Search of a Soul*, p. 179.

[11]*Contributions to Analytical Psychology*, p. 235.

[12]*Modern Man in Search of a Soul*, p. 179.

[13]*Contributions to Analytical Psychology*, pp. 235/6.

[14]*Ibid.* It is curious to note, in passing, that this particular point is completely misinter-

preted and misrepresented in a popular work on Jung, *The Psychology of C. G. Jung,* by Jolande Jacobi. (New Haven: Yale University Press, 1954, p. 35.)

Section 3
[15]*Ibid.,* p. 238. (Italics mine.)
[16]*Ibid.,* p. 243.

Section 4
[17]*Modern Man in Search of a Soul,* p. 180.
[18]*Ibid.*
[19]*Contributions to Analytical Psychology,* p. 241.
[20]*Modern Man ...,* p. 184.
[21]*Contributions to Analytical Psychology,* p. 248.
[22]*Modern Man ...,* p. 190.
[23]*Contributions to Analytical Psychology,* p. 246.
[24]*Modern Man ...,* p. 188.
[25]*Contributions ...,* p. 247.
[26]*Modern Man ...,* p. 188.
[27]*Contributions ...,* p. 246.
[28]*Modern Man ...,* pp. 190/1. (Italics mine.)
[29]*Contributions ...,* p. 248. (Italics mine.)
[30]*Modern Man ...,* p. 189.
[31]*Contributions ...,* p. 248.

Section 5
[32]*Modern Man ...,* p. 194. (Italics mine.)
[33]*Ibid.,* p. 195. (Italics mine.)
[34]*Ibid.,* p. 195. It should be noted that in the case of the former "classes" the collective factors function in consciousness, whereas, in the case of the artist the collective psy-

chic life refers to the collective *unconscious.*

PART III
Section 1
[1]Sigmund Freud, *Collected Papers Volume IV,* London; Hogarth Press & the International Psychoanalytical Library, 1925, p. 109.
[2]C. G. Jung, essay entitled "The Spirit of Psychology," in *Spirit and Nature,* New York: Pantheon Books, 1954, p. 389.
[3]C. G. Jung, *Modern Man in Search of a Soul,* New York: Harcourt Brace & Co., 1933, p. 190.
[4]C. G. Jung, *Psychological Types,* London: Routledge & Kegan Paul, 1953, p. 556.
[5]Written in 1920.
[6]Sigmund Freud, *Beyond the Pleasure Principle,* New York: Liveright, 1950, p. 83.
[7]Edward Glover, *Freud or Jung?,* New York: Meridian Books, 1957.
[8]*Ibid.,* p. 50.
[9]*Ibid.,* p. 46.
[10]*Ibid.,* p. 35.
[11]*Ibid,* p. 37.
[12]*Ibid.,* pp. 41/2.
[13]*Ibid.,* p. 42. (Italics mine.)
[14]*Ibid.,* p. 51. (Italics mine.)
[15]Melville J. Herskovits, *Man and His Works,* New York: Alfred A. Knopf, 1956, p. 47.
[16]*Ibid.,* Chapter 15. pp. 229-240.
[17]*Ibid.,* p. 233. (Italics mine.)
[18]*Ibid,,* p. 378.
[19]*Ibid.,* p. 380.

[20]*Ibid.*, p. 27.

Section 2

[21]Abraham Kaplan, "Freud and Modern Philosophy,"in *Freud and the 20th Century*, New York: Meridian, 1957.

[22]Lionel Trilling, "Art and Neurosis," in *The Liberal Imagination*, New York: Viking, 1950.

[23]Ludwig Marcuse, "Freud's Aesthetics," in *The Journal of Aesthetics*, September, 1958.

[24]Kaplan, *op. cit.*, pp. 216/7. (Italics mine.)

[25]Trilling, *op cit.*, p. 161. (Italics mine.)

[26]Marcuse, *op. cit.*, p. 8.

[27]Sigmund Freud, "The Relation of the Poet to Daydreaming," *Collected Papers*, Vol. IV, London: The Hogarth Press, 1950, p. 182.

[28]*Ibid.*, p. 183.

[29]*Ibid.*

[30]Marcuse, *op. cit.*, p. 6.

[31]Freud, *The Future of an Illusion*, New York: Doubleday Anchor Books, 1957, p. 19.

[32]*Ibid.*, p. 19.

[33]Freud, *Civilization and Its Discontents*, London: The Hogarth Press, 1951, p. 25.

[34]Ernst Kris, *Psychoanalytic Explorations in Art*, New York: International Universities Press, 1952, p. 13. (Italics mine). It is interesting to notice that in this extensive study there is no interpretation offered of "symbolism" as such, and the adjective "symbolical" is applied to only children's play and fairy tales.

[35]Marcuse, *op. cit.*, p. 7.

[36]*Ibid.*, p. 11.

[37]Frederick J. Hacker, "On Artistic Productions," in *Explorations in Psychoanalysis*, ed. Robert Lindner, New York: Julian Press, 1953, p. 129.

[38]Marcuse, *op. cit.*, p. 11.

[39]Sir Herbert Read, "Poetic Consciousness and Creative Experience" in *Eranos Yearbook, 1956*, Zürich: Rhein Verlag, 1956, pp. 382/3.

[40]Jung, *Modern Man in Seach of a Soul*, p. 179.

[41]Jung, *Contributions to Analytical Psychology*, p. 245.

[42]*Ibid.*, p. 245. (Italics mine.)

[43]See Part 2, Section 4.

[44]Irving Babbitt, *Rousseau and Romanticism*, New York: Meridian Books, 1955, p. 27.

[45]*Ibid., p.* 29.

[46]*Ibid.*

[47]Jacques Barzun, *Romanticism and the Modern Ego*, Boston: Little, Brown & Co., 1947, p. 96.

[48]Lionel Trilling, "The Meaning of a Literary Idea," *op. cit.*, p. 284.

[49]D. H. Lawrence, *Selested Essays, London*s Penguin Books, 1950, p. 268.

[50]Jung, *Contributions to Analytical Psychology*, p. 241.

[51]*Ibid.*

[52]See Bibliography.

[53]Glover, *op. cit.*, p. 169.

⁵⁴*Ibid.*, p. 169.

⁵⁵William York Tindall, *The Literary Symbol*, Blooming-ton Indiana University Press, 1955, p. 6.

Section 3

⁵⁶Ira Progoff, *Jung's Psychology and Its Social Meaning*, New York: Grove Press, 1953, p. 281.

⁵⁷*Ibid.*, p. 187.

⁵⁸Sigmund Freud, *Beyond the Pleasure Principle*, p. 72.

⁵⁹Edward Glover, *Freud or Jung?*, p. 173.

⁶⁰Ernest Cassirer, *An Essay on Man*, New Haven: Yale University Press, 1944, p. 25. (Italics mine.)

⁶¹Edward Glover, *Freud or Jung?*, p. 174.

⁶²*Ibid.*

Index of Proper Names